# Nudge, Nudge, Think, Think

# Nudge, Nudge, Think, Think

## Experimenting with Ways to Change Civic Behaviour

Peter John, Sarah Cotterill, Alice Moseley,
Liz Richardson, Graham Smith,
Gerry Stoker and Corinne Wales

BLOOMSBURY

LONDON • NEW DELHI • NEW YORK • SYDNEY

**Bloomsbury Academic**
An imprint of Bloomsbury Publishing Plc

| 50 Bedford Square | 175 Fifth Avenue |
|---|---|
| London | New York |
| WC1B 3DP | NY 10010 |
| UK | USA |

www.bloomsbury.com

First published 2011
This revised paperback edition published 2013

Cover designer – Hugh Adams, AB3 Design
Cover image: Artwork/Image permissions information

**British Library Cataloguing-in-Publication Data**
A catalogue record for this book is available from the British Library.

ISBN: HB: 978-1-8496-6059-4
PB: 978-1-7809-3555-3
eBook: 978-1-84966-058-7 (ebook)

**Library of Congress Cataloging-in-Publication Data**
A catalog record for this book is available from the Library of Congress

Printed and bound by CPI Group (UK) Ltd, Croydon, CR0 4YY

# Preface to the Paperback Edition

It is just over a year and half since *Nudge, Nudge, Think, Think: Using Experiments to Change Civic Behaviour* first appeared in print – and we presented our final research findings at a public event near Whitehall as long ago as June 2010. Much has happened since. Nudge has moved from the newsrooms and features pages into the heart of the policy process. Whereas in 2010 one of the authors of the book *Nudge: Improving Decisions About Health, Wealth, and Happiness*, Richard Thaler, regularly appeared on radio programmes, such as BBC Radio 4 Today, advertising his book and regaling anecdotes, now there are more policies that use nudge as an integral part of their design. In other words nudge has moved from being an idea promoted on the airwaves to policies designed to encourage citizens to change their behaviour.

The UK Liberal Democrat-Conservative coalition government, which came into office in May 2010, takes a strong interest in nudge, partly because the Prime Minister, David Cameron, is keen to address societal problems. As a result the government set up the Behavioural Insights Team, based in the Cabinet Office, to help formulate behavioural interventions. The 'nudge unit' attracted a skeptical press at its start, but the critics were won over after it secured a number of early successes that showed both the use of behavioural insights and the saving of money, such as sending texts to the mobile telephones of those who have outstanding court fines. The team promotes the use of randomized controlled trials to evaluate policy interventions, which involves varying what government does. To this end the unit published *Test, Learn Adapt: Developing Public Policy with Randomised Controlled Trials* (2012), by Laura Haynes, Owain Service, Ben Goldacre and David Torgerson, to encourage good practice. What should not be underestimated is the extent to which the experimental and behavioural agendas have carried forward in central government as a whole, and this extends to public agencies, local government and recently to the voluntary sector.

We should not be too distracted by the policies of the coalition: there is an appetite for behaviour change policies worldwide that comes from all sides of the political spectrum. For example, President Obama appointed Cass Sunstein, one of the authors of *Nudge*, to head up the Office of Information and Regulatory Affairs. Then in France, the Centre for Strategic Analysis of the Prime Minister employed a behaviour science expert, Olivier Oullier, as an advisor on behaviour change policies. The Scottish Government has carried out a review of the international evidence for behaviour change initiatives. The Behavioural Insights Team now works directly with the New South Wales government in Australia and the Danish government has proposed a mandated choice for organ donation.

If policy-makers are increasingly in love with nudge, those in the academy have produced a more critical commentary, perhaps alarmed at its success in the political world. The economist Robert Sugden in 'On Nudging' (*International Journal of the Economics of Business*, 2009, vol. 16, issue 3, pp. 365–73) has attacked the claims of libertarian paternalism on the ground that nudge is not consistent with liberty; recently the political theorist Andrew Dobson in 'Nudging and environmental citizenship (http://www.ethicsandtechnology. eu/blog/post/nudging_environmental_citizenship/) considers nudge to be another symptom of the death of politics, an idea that can be harnessed for any technocratic purpose. The House of Lords Science and Technology Sub-Committee I Inquiry *Behaviour Change* (2011) drew attention to the limitations of nudge in addressing powerful social problems, such as obesity. Similarly, Theresa Marteau and colleagues in 'Judging Nudging: can 'nudging' improve population health? The *British Medical Journal* (29 January 2011, vol. 342) argues that more evidence is needed on whether nudges are effective in achieving the sustained behaviour change required for improved health outcomes. Peter John and Liz Richardson in *Nudging Citizens Towards Localism* (British Academy, 2011) suggest that policy-makers have not reconciled the centralist implications of behaviour change policies with policies of localism and decentralization. The debate continues.

Our book goes beyond nudge too. In *Nudge, Nudge, Think, Think*, we argue a greater attention to 'think' might address the potential crisis of legitimacy that behaviour change policies can suffer from. The involvement of citizens in debate has the potential to offer a solution for governments in their search for more legitimacy for their policies. Nudge works best when there is a shared consensus about expected behaviours for policies areas like tax, recycling, donating to charity, voting and local volunteering, which are widely viewed as the right thing to do. Think offers an alternative strategy to nudge in circumstances where society is deeply divided on an issue, such as over energy or transport policy for example. In these situations, how else is it possible to achieve behaviour change other than through widespread debate and reflection? It is true that policy-makers in England have paid less attention to think, which was embraced by the Labour government 1997–2010 with its appetite for consultation and deliberative forums; but the interest continues elsewhere in the world (see www.participedia.net). Think is needed now more than ever.

# Foreword

The Rt Hon Greg Clark MP
Financial Secretary to the Treasury, former minister
for Planning and Decentralization

The Big Society is based on a simple idea: that Britain derives its strength not solely from the actions of government, but from the ingenuity of individuals and communities, entrepreneurs and volunteers – men and women who contribute, in a myriad of different ways, to the nation's prosperity and well-being. And in much the same way that government alone is not responsible for the nation's triumphs and successes, government alone cannot provide the whole solution to many of the challenges we face as a society. Our ability to meet the challenges of climate change, for instance, hinges to a significant extent on individuals' willingness to alter their lifestyle and cut their carbon footprint. Or take public health. The degree to which today's 30-year-olds choose to eat well and exercise regularly will have a profound impact on the demands on the National Health Service in the future. The difference between success and failure – between obesity and good health, between sustainable consumption and a carbon binge – lies in how people decide to act, individually and collectively. In other words, making Britain a better place to live depends on each of us changing our behaviour.

The question is: What can government do for its part to encourage responsible, altruistic and civic-minded behaviour? For decades now, successive administrations of different political affiliations have sought to achieve social policy objectives by pulling on the levers of central power. Whether the aim was to curb anti-social behaviour, improve health or encourage recycling, the standard approach to policy-making went something like this: a group of experts was convened in Whitehall to discuss the problem; civil servants summarized the consensus in the room about what were considered the most effective solutions; they codified those solutions into a set of 'best practice'; public services everywhere were mandated, by means of legislation, guidance or inspection, to put that best practice into effect. This approach is often referred to as 'centralism'.

The argument put forward by the proponents of centralism has always been that it represents a means of enforcing minimum standards and making struggling services buck up their ideas. But there is a growing recognition today, not only that centralism has reached the point of diminishing returns, but also that, in some cases, an excess of central control has done harm. It has created costly bureaucracy; distorted the way public services are delivered; and sought to impose nationally designed solutions, whereas Britain's communities are astonishingly diverse in their needs and natures.

Crucially, when it comes to the subtle question of behaviour change, centralism often presents an all-too-rigid answer. In cases of totally unacceptable and unethical behaviour, centrally determined legislation and punishment are perfectly appropriate; I doubt whether any of us would seriously object to strong criminal sanctions against murder or fraud. A measure of central prescription may also be an appropriate means of dissuading some specific types of harmful behaviour – I'm personally in favour of the ban on smoking in public places, for example. But much of the time, and in many areas of policy, simply telling people what to do can be wholly counterproductive, especially at a time when deference is low and mistrust of politicians and civil servants is high.

Take housing policy. As a growing nation, Britain needs more homes. In the noughties, government sought to get those homes built by setting national and regional targets. But people bridled at the imposition; and the effect of targets was not to increase house-building rates but to entrench local opposition to new building. Some of the old Regional Spatial Strategies that contained the targets attracted literally thousands of critical responses. The tragedy is that the default response in some places is now to resist any development at all costs, including new homes which families need, office space which would support new businesses and jobs, and municipal buildings which could be the neighbourhood's crowning glory.

In other cases, the mere threat of heavy-handed attempts by officialdom to do the right thing by enforcing a standard of behaviour – for example, punishing people for the incorrect use of recycling bins – has diminished people's appetite to take control for themselves and sapped their enthusiasm to play their part.

The bottom line is that policy-makers need a broader range of tools than the hammer of direction and instruction. They need to find more intelligent and more effective ways to encourage responsible behaviour by individuals and communities.

This represents a major challenge to parts of the policy-making machine in Whitehall and town halls alike. When pulling the old central levers of power is deep in the muscle memory, it can be hard to let go. But government at all levels needs to get better at engaging in a proper conversation with communities; giving them information, not rules; incentives, not diktats.

Instead of telling people what to do in response to social, environmental or economic challenges, we need to get better at giving them the space to make up their own minds, and asking them what they think the solutions should be. It's an approach which has its roots in assuming the best of people, and in their ability to be rational, generous and fair.

I greatly welcome, therefore, the work that the authors of this book have carried out to analyse the effectiveness of a range of different approaches to encouraging responsible behaviour – from the 'nudge' of giving cues and signals, introducing small incentives and harnessing the power of peer pressure, to the 'think' of providing people with information and asking them to reflect on the evidence before making choices. This book's great strength is that it gives practical and tangible examples of the benefits and shortcomings of a variety of different approaches, and looks at a broad range of different policies and scenarios, with examples including organ donation and voting, and locations ranging from suburbs to urban estates.

As the authors themselves make clear, it is still early days for the exploration and analysis of these different methods of changing behaviours, and the research raises questions as well as answers: How significant are the changes encouraged by these techniques? Are these changes transitory, or sustained? Does investing in nudge and think represent an effective use of public money compared to other methods? And does government need to seek public consent for the more widespread use of such techniques?

The main finding, however, is crystal clear: public bodies can, when they put their minds to it, work with communities in different, less directive, more effective ways to deliver behaviour change in the wider interest of society. Adapting to different ways of working will, I suspect, be a steep learning curve for many policy-makers. For the light that it sheds on the path ahead, this book is both timely and welcome.

# The Authors

**Peter John** is Professor of Political Science and Public Policy at University College London. He previously held the Hallsworth Chair of Governance at the University of Manchester, where he co-directed the Institute of Political and Economic Governance (IPEG). His books include *Analysing Public Policy* (2nd edition 2012) and *Making Policy Work* (2011).

**Sarah Cotterill** works at the University of Manchester and is an adviser for the NIHR Research Design Service. She has a PhD from the University of Leeds on *Partnership Working in Local Electronic Government* and she has many years of work experience in housing and community regeneration.

**Alice Moseley** is a Research Fellow in the Department of Politics at the University of Exeter. She was previously at the University of Southampton where she was part of the *Rediscovering the Civic* project team. She has published on a variety of public policy topics, including joined-up government and evidence-based policy. She is currently working on an Economic and Social Research Council research project on succession outcomes in UK government executive agencies.

**Liz Richardson** is a Research Fellow at the Institute of Political and Economic Governance (IPEG), University of Manchester. She has conducted research on community self-help, local representative democracy and the re-design of public services, working with policy makers in local and central government and the voluntary sector, as well as hundreds of community organizations. She is the author of *DIY Community Action* (2008) and a Director of the National Communities Resource Centre, a charity which supports community volunteers.

**Graham Smith** is Professor of Politics in the Centre for Citizenship, Globalization and Governance (C2G2) and the Third Sector Research Centre (TSRC) at the University of Southampton. His research interests include democratic theory and practice, environmental politics and the social economy. His most recent book is *Democratic Innovations: Designing Institutions for Citizen Participation* (2009).

**Gerry Stoker** is Professor of Politics and Governance at the University of Southampton, and Director of the Centre for Citizenship, Globalization and Governance (C2G2). His most recent book is *Governance Theory and Practice: a Cross Disciplinary Approach* (2010, with Vasudha Chhotray).

**Corinne Wales** is Visiting Fellow at the Centre for Citizenship, Globalization and Governance (C2G2), University of Southampton, where she was part of the *Rediscovering the Civic* project team. She has conducted research on deliberative democratic theory and practice, the institutionalization of trust in public policy, risk communication and citizen behaviour change.

# Acknowledgements

This book comes out of a research project that took place between September 2007 and June 2010 called 'Rediscovering the Civic: Achieving Better Outcomes in Public Policy', which was supported by the UK Economic and Social Research Council (ESRC), the Department of Communities and Local Government (CLG) and the North West Improvement and Efficiency Partnership (NWIEP) (RES-177-25-0002). We first thank the funders for giving us the opportunity to engage in such an interesting and relevant piece of work, applying the experimental method to study public participation in the UK for the first time. It was a big act of faith by our government co-sponsors in a relatively slow-moving project. In spite of the time it took us to complete our work, we believe that the findings are as relevant as ever as the UK government sets out on a programme of work to promote the Big Society. Our particular gratitude goes to Paul McCafferty, then head of Local Governance Research Unit at CLG, who helped organize the finance for the project. We are also very grateful to the team at CLG for their assistance throughout, in particular Arianna Haberis and Wendy Russell Barter.

We would like to thank the members of the advisory group to the project, who gave of their time so freely: Matthew Taylor, Chris Wyatt, Arianna Haberis, Mike Saward, Henry Tam, Joyce Redfern, Barry Quirk, Shamitt Saggar, Lawrence Pratchett and Jane Martin. We also thank those who spoke at our final event on the 23 June 2010, in particular Philip Blond, Toby Blume, Sue Goss and the Minister for Planning and Decentralization, Greg Clark MP, as well as members of the advisory group.

We owe a great debt to our administrator, Margaret Holmes, who coped so well in organizing such a complex and multifaceted project, especially its finances and sub-contracts, and who helped make the final event such a success. We are especially thankful to the researchers who worked alongside us, in particular Hanhua Liu, Tessa Brannan and Hisako Nomura. Hanhua contributed to the first recycling randomized controlled trial and on our separately reported survey work. Tessa worked with Peter John on the original Wythenshawe Get Out the Vote experiment reported in Chapter 4. Hisako worked on the analysis of the deliberation project and came up with the food waste feedback experiment idea and led this part of our work, which we report in Chapter 3. We are very pleased that Helen Margetts collaborated with us on the research that forms the basis for Chapter 6, and we thank both Tobias Escher and Stéphane Reissfelder for their energy and ingenuity in planning and organizing the experiments at the Oxford Internet

Institute. Patrick Sturgis also contributed his impressive skills to the statistical work on our deliberation project. We are grateful to Ben Smith and David Torgerson, who carried out many of the randomizations, in this way being the neutral third parties for this essential task. Don Green has been an inspiration, and we thank him in particular for spending a whole afternoon with us brainstorming our putative experiments and for commenting on the manuscript.

It was great news that Bloomsbury Academic was keen on us from the start and we are very flattered to be at the forefront of its online publishing experiment. We thank Frances Pinter for her support for the project. In particular, we benefited from Caroline Wintersgill's enthusiasm and input throughout, especially her very helpful suggestions after reading the draft manuscript. We also appreciated the thoughtful comments of the publisher's anonymous reviewer. We are grateful to Kay Caldwell of Clere Story, who edited the manuscript for us, and to the copyeditors at Bloomsbury, in particular Howard Watson. We also benefited from the feedback of students on City University's Publishing MA, who were assigned the book as a project in the digitization and publishing module, and who asked Peter John a number of probing and useful questions about the enterprise.

We would like to thank the many people who helped deliver our projects in local government, the National Health Service and the voluntary sector. We thank all those at EMERGE – in particular Lucy Danger, Mark Hill, Denise Lambert, Sebastian Serayet, Jo-Anne Witcombe – who provided invaluable ideas and practical support with the recycling and food waste experiments, and Mark Husdan from Oldham Council's waste team who worked closely with us on the food waste experiment, plus all the monitors and canvassers who worked on the projects. We gratefully acknowledge the work of Isobel McVicar at Community HEART, staff at Manchester City Council, all the people who staffed the drop-off points and the colleagues and volunteers (Tessa Brannan, Bethan Harries and Liz Pool) who helped sort the large number of books that arrived at the Institute for Political and Economic Governance's office as part of the pledging project. We are deeply appreciative to the staff at Ipsos MORI, in particular Lisa Valade-DeMelo, who helped us deliver the online deliberation which was leap into the unknown in designing a new kind of intervention. The company calmly complied with what may have seemed like endless requests to redesign the project. We would also like to thank Greg Naughton who filmed the videos that were used for the online forums and Julie Martin and Niki Lewis who worked so well with our design experiment in Wiltshire, and Share D'All, formerly of Hampshire County

Council. Mike Amos-Smith of stories4change was a partner in the Building Links project, and gave over and above, including making YouTube videos and insightful comments. We also thank the eight courageous community groups who lobbied councillors with us.

For the volunteering experiment, we have huge admiration for our risk-taking local authority colleagues in Blackburn with Darwen Borough Council: Peter Little, Billy Maxwell (now Liverpool Council), Ross McQueen, Geoff Cole, Lesley Fox (the frontline worker) and Tanya Gallagher. Special thanks go to Sarah Henry (now Manchester Council) for being one of our supporters throughout. Our thanks also go to NHS Blood and Transplant for advice and assistance with our two organ donation experiments, particularly Angie Burton, Christine Cole, Rachel Dance and Professor James Neuberger, and again to Ipsos MORI who also helped conduct our online organ donation experiment. We appreciate the contributions of the postgraduate research assistants and the students involved in the university-based experiment.

Finally, we owe a debt of gratitude to the citizens themselves who participated in our project, and who showed they were willing to donate organs, recycle waste, vote and volunteer in response to our prompts and interventions.

# Contents

# Figures

# Tables

# Introduction

We start with an example. In 2008 the environment department of an English local council near to Manchester faced a problem: how to get a group of citizens to recycle more of their household waste. This well-run authority, with considerable green credentials, wanted to do more for the environment. It had already been very successful in persuading many residents, particularly those who live in the detached houses and terraces in the borough, to separate their waste. But very little recycling was happening on some of its publicly owned housing estates, where many tenants made little attempt to sort out their rubbish into cans, glass and paper. Instead, they put all their waste into refuse sacks and deposited them in the general waste collection bins. There was even one small estate where no recycling was happening at all.

To try to get the message to the residents on this problem estate, the council's officers sent leaflets to each of its households, and then put up large, colourful posters at the entrances to the buildings and on the walkways. But these acts of encouragement had no effect. In the end the officers became so frustrated they instructed the waste collection service not to pick up the rubbish for a few weeks. The idea was that if the people living the estate saw the growing pile of refuse sacks they would be shamed into recycling. Instead of picking up the rubbish in the normal away, the refuse collectors placed the sacks in the central grassed areas of the estate in full view of everyone. Over the weeks that followed, these courtyards became filled up with black refuse bags (the council regularly checked there was no public health problem).

Well, what happened? Did the good citizens of the estate start placing glass, cans and paper into their respective collection boxes? The simple answer is no. They ignored the message from the council. In the end the environment department gave up and the garbage trucks returned to their normal cycle of visits, and collected the black plastic bags with their unsorted waste. The plain fact is that modern government with its complex laws, access to finance, public relations/marketing skills, professionally trained employees and information technology capacity – as well as the leverage it gets from democratic legitimacy – cannot get a group of citizens to behave differently if they do not wish to do so.

The story shows there are limits to what government can achieve with its conventional means of bringing about change. It cannot command people to be more neighbourly or to save for their retirement, or to volunteer to help out in their community or – in this case – to make a contribution to the environment by recycling more of what they dispose. The kinds of problems that many societies now need to solve require changing the behaviour of citizens, whose private actions are hard to regulate by laws and commands. And even if these top-down tools of government worked, there are some moral qualms about using them too much. Citizens in Western industrial democracies have come to value their individual freedoms, lifestyle choices and their right to have a say. They are less deferential, less automatically inclined to accept the claimed wisdom of experts and more willing to challenge those in authority. Modern citizens want to be active choosers, or at least as much as they can be, and as a result commands or crass incentives to change their behaviour are less likely to be effective and to be acceptable. The use of laws and commands, which was the normal reflex action of policy-makers in previous years, is no longer such an attractive option.

It is possible for governments to provide incentives to support new behaviours, but the money that governments spend only comes from taxpayers, and to tackle the full range of social and economic issues would require public spending at levels that would be unsustainable. As the adverse state of public spending and the cutbacks in spending in many Western industrial nations indicate, the matching of revenues with spending – at least in the long run – is one the oldest lessons of effective government.

But there are alternatives: what may be called the softer tools of government. These involve working more closely with the citizens, understanding how they are thinking and encouraging them to take – and to own – better decisions. It would involve a 'nudge' rather than a push or a shout, and would incorporate a 'think', that is government and other public bodies allowing the citizens to debate and to deliberate so they can decide what is best. We aim in this book to find out whether these alternatives can work.

Nudges are about framing choices. Citizens now live in a complex world with many signals about what is the best thing to do. Given that people have only a limited amount of time to process all the information coming from this world, they use social cues to help them decide what to do: Will it take much effort to change behaviour? What are other citizens doing? Can they work out the impact of a shift in behaviour quickly and easily? Governments, working in cooperation with citizens, can help shape the multiple daily choices people make in ways that could be better for society and its citizens if these social cues are right.

Think refers to another broad set of tools – stretching from consultation to handing over decisions to citizens – which have become prominently and widely established in the world of governance over the last few decades. Broadly, these multiple forms of public engagement rest on the assumption that citizens – given the right evidence, enough time and an appropriate context – can come to the best judgement about what is good for them and their fellow citizens, and then take action as a result. Solutions can be found to challenging issues, and the pathways to behaviour change can be illuminated and smoothed, because citizens have been involved in the construction of the answer. Both the legitimacy and likely effectiveness of any solution are thus increased, and its chances of being adopted are maximized.

This book is about these softer tools of intervention and it asks two questions: What are the underlying mechanisms that these tools depend on? And will policies that use them work – that is, will their use lead to changes in behaviour that bring public benefit or value? In answering these questions, the book breaks new ground. It is one of the first accounts of these new tools of governance and at the same time seeks to find out whether they work or not. There are plenty of books that advocate the use of new kinds of public management by government, starting from Osborne and Gaebler's *Rethinking Government* (Osborne and Gaebler 1993) with its famous dictum that government should do more steering and less rowing (more commissioning and less direct provision). Central and local governments have been quick to adopt this kind of thinking, as they have the newer doctrines of behavioural economics and nudge. The appearance in 10 Downing Street of Richard Thaler, one of the authors of the book *Nudge* (Thaler and Sunstein 2008), is an indication of the intellectual fashions of the moment. Many local councils, such as West Sussex, have signed up to the project of behaviour change. The other author of *Nudge*, Cass Sunstein, heads up the US Office of Information and Regulatory Affairs.

We are able to offer something different from these entreaties: an analysis of the underlying thinking behind the most prominent new forms of intervention. Whilst supporting many of the nudge initiatives, we argue that think should complement them and will deepen and broaden out the behaviour-change programme. Think helps deal with the potential lack of legitimacy of nudge and its appearance of being manipulative. In general terms, nudgers should consider incorporating some elements of think into their interventions.

Most of all, and uniquely, we provide a systematic and rigorous approach to the study of the effectiveness of both nudge and think. This book reports the first attempt in the UK to show how randomized controlled trials can reveal what works when it comes to changing citizen behaviour. Experiments allow a reliable inference to be made between a cause and its effect. When it comes to introducing new medicines in Western industrial democracies it is expected that they will be the focus of rigorous randomized controlled trails before they are introduced. That is, the research measures the difference between a sample of the population who receive the treatment and those in a control group who do not receive the intervention. The same logic of testing should be applied to interventions in the non-medical field and specifically when governments are trying to change civic behaviour. Policy-makers can construct simple randomized controlled trials or experiments to test what forms of nudge might work or what forms of think-based interventions are efficacious. So our book not only offers particular examples of interventions that have made a difference, but it makes a case for a general approach to testing what works that is rigorous and achievable. In cooperation with thousands of citizens and dozens of local governments, community groups and non-profits, we have been trialling practices and ideas about how to stimulate different kinds of civic behaviour and this book reports the findings.

## Plan of the book

We spend the first part of the book examining nudge and think, before setting out our preferred methods of investigating them: randomized controlled trials and design experiments. In Chapter 1, 'Nudging and Thinking', we discuss nudge and think in some depth. We explore the assumptions of nudge and think strategies and what they can offer to the challenge of stimulating civic behaviour. We also engage with normative questions about whether the state or other public agencies should nudge citizens or encourage them to think. Chapter 2 is called 'Testing', and is about how to find out what works. We argue that policy-makers and others should adopt an experimental approach when they do not know the answer about how to achieve their goals. The randomized controlled trial and its qualitative cousin, the design experiment, provide robust methods that can ascertain whether interventions designed to improve civic behaviour work or not. So, in Chapters 1 and 2, we set out the main message of the book: policy-makers should experiment to find the most effective way of encouraging better civic behaviour.

The second and more substantial part of the book is about the key outcomes that policy-makers are interested in, and this part reports and discusses experiments aimed at shaping civic behaviour. We start out looking at mostly nudge-based strategies and then examine some think interventions. These empirical chapters examine some of the existing evidence (both observational and experimental), provide tests of our original and innovative interventions in different areas of civic behaviour and come to judgements about what is the state of the current understanding of how best to stimulate civic behaviour.

Each of the empirical chapters takes a similar structure: we first explain why we should study this topic, whether it is recycling, donating or another activity; we review what is already known about it; we describe the interventions and convey what we have found out. Finally, we set out the lessons for nudge or think and recommend additional literature so the reader may explore the topic further.

Chapter 3, 'Recycling', is about how to encourage household recycling of waste. A detailed case is presented of a nudge strategy that involved canvassing people on their doorsteps, encouraging them to recycle their waste and comparing the results with a randomized controlled trial. The findings show the strength of nudge in that the canvassing increases recycling, but it also shows the weakness of nudge as the effect reduces three months later. The chapter contains a second experiment that examines the role of feedback in encouraging recycling. The chapter concludes with a discussion of the implications of these findings for the advocates of the nudge strategy.

Chapter 4 is entitled 'Volunteering'. Here we review the evidence on promoting volunteering and asks what a nudge strategy could offer. The chapter contains details on a design experiment that asks citizens complaining to a local authority telephone call centre to undertake some civic-minded acts. What do these findings indicate about the challenge of promoting volunteering? By changing the choice architecture, is it possible to turn complainers to volunteers?

In Chapter 5, 'Voting', we show how experiments can test a variety of strategies for mobilizing the vote in a Get Out the Vote campaign. There is a vast literature on getting citizens to engage politically, but could nudge offer some additional insights? We report on an experimental intervention about how to get citizens to vote and reflect on its implications for stimulating civic behaviour more generally.

Chapter 6 is about another individual political civic behaviour: signing a petition, a simple and powerful way for the voice of the citizen to be heard by those in power. In 'Petitioning' we report on an experiment that seeks to manipulate the information that people receive when making an e-petition. We seek to find out whether allowing people to view the number of other e-petitioners affects their willingness to sign.

Chapter 7 is about 'Giving' and asks if a nudge, through creating psychological pressure to do something, can encourage people to follow through their good intention to give to charity. The experimenters asked people to pledge to give a book from their home to help children in Africa.

In Chapter 8, 'Donating', we discuss an experiment about donating organs. We ask whether the nudge strategy of changing the choice architecture can encourage people to agree to donate their organs after their death. We then outline a second experiment testing whether a booklet alone or a booklet combined with a discussion (think) would cause people to be more willing to donate their organs. In this experiment, we are able to test elements of think and nudge together.

Chapter 9 is called 'Debating'. The idea of deliberation is well established as a think strategy. But can it deal with controversial issues of public policy in an online environment? This chapter reviews the literature on this subject and reports a unique experiment in large-scale online deliberation involving 6,000 citizens. Drawing on evidence from these online debates on community cohesion and youth anti-social behaviour, we show how online engagement can influence knowledge and opinions about public policy options.

In Chapter 10, 'Including', we find out how public authorities use media technology (in this case a DVD) to raise the profile of excluded voices as part of a decentralization initiative. The design experiment highlights the crucial, but difficult, role of facilitation, in particular the impact it can have in creating more inclusive dialogue.

Chapter 11 is titled 'Linking', and is about the wider institutional context of public decision-making, which may need to be reformed if think is going to work. Thinking requires linking, and only makes sense if the ideas that citizens come up with are reviewed and judged openly by the policy-makers. Why participate if no one is listening? This chapter presents findings about how citizens link to government that reveal the extent of the gap between citizens and local representatives. It may be the case that the difficulty of linking elites to citizens is the central flaw of the think strategy. We report the results of an experiment that tests how responsive policy-makers are to requests from a citizen's interest group.

In the conclusion, 'Experimenting with Ways to Change Civic Behaviour', we bring the insights from the various chapters together, and draw out the implications for policy-makers. It is here we make the case for more experiments to understand what drives civic behaviour and to find out the best way governments can intervene to promote it and thereby achieve better policy outcomes. We advocate a local and decentralized approach to citizen involvement and behaviour change that reflects how we applied the experimental method and the way we used partnerships with local interest groups and public bodies to develop a genuinely creative and evidence-based form of local policy-making. In this way, the leverage of nudge and creative potential of think can be brought together.

## Defining the good citizen

Before getting to the core argument about think and nudge, and our tests of what tools drive changes in citizen behaviour, we need to address a prior question: what kind of behaviour should governments and public agencies be encouraging? This is not a straightforward question to answer, for what makes for good civic behaviour is temporal, unfixed and dynamic. The good citizen of Athenian democracy was one skilled in the art of soldiering, the twenty-first-century good citizen might visit their elderly neighbour, engage in making decisions about local public spending or help support their local park management committee. Civic behaviour can manifest itself in several ways (John, Fieldhouse and Liu 2011). We can think of examples of individual political action where individuals seek to influence decision-making through signing a petition or voting in elections. Also familiar is the practice of collective political action, where people work together to influence decision-making, perhaps in a community meeting to think through a tricky issue that seeks to define priorities and actions for an area. We can also recognize many examples of citizens adopting a Do-it-Yourself attitude and practice, when individuals act in the wider public interest, for example by driving an elderly person to the doctor, recycling household waste or volunteering to do hospital visits. There are also collective forms of this kind of civic behaviour which could include being a member of a community group to clean up a local park, forming a social enterprise to run a community facility or pledging to exchange favours formally via a time-bank (Richardson 2008). For this reason, governments and public agencies need to recognize a wider set of behaviours than they have done hitherto.

Having established what kinds of behaviour are important to encourage, what are the main motivators of civic action that we need to establish before intervening with experiments? Each individual will have potentially multiple motivations for engaging in civic behaviour, some more self-oriented and some more regarding of others. For example, people who volunteer may be interested in helping their neighbours; or they do it out of loyalty to the area; or because their friends are involved and asked them; or they turn up to community events because they want to meet people and make new friends. Others may enjoy the challenge of getting a project off the ground and winning against the odds; or some may see it as a route to employment in the third sector. Individuals may have one reason or many, which may vary according the task involved. Engaging in civic action can be about protecting a person's interests, or those of others, or can be about both.

Civic behaviour requires effort. Exercising self-restraint and personal responsibility, becoming informed about issues that affect communities and participating in consultations and changing entrenched habits for collective ends all demand considerable exertion by individuals. The basic idea is that to have the society that people want, they need to agree to give more back, which has been echoed in statements from people as diverse as Bill Gates and Barack Obama. But voluntary acts might not happen without some external support and intervention. Of course, there are some self-organizing activities, such as neighbourhood support, families whose members care for each other and various forms of local organizing, such as petitioning and campaigning; but in many cases actions will not take place effectively and on a large enough scale without some intervention by an external agency. Most people engage civically in many ways in their lives. Citizens do things individually and we do things collectively. The scale of civic behaviour is already substantial but people could do more if we were approached in the right way. At least that it the proposition we aim to test in this book.

1

# Nudging and Thinking

What is a nudge strategy and what is a think strategy? In this chapter we compare and contrast these approaches to changing civic behaviour. We argue that even though the two strategies draw on different traditions of research, they are both a response to a shared understanding of the human predicament, which is that people are boundedly rational. Individuals seek to economize on the use of information, even when seeking to reflect on big problems of the day as well as when deciding to carry out a routine civic action.

We then ask whether policy-makers should be trying to stimulate civic behaviour. Are efforts to involve citizens more in public life too paternalistic and limiting of individual freedom? What people do in civil society, it could be argued, is up to them and is not for the state to dictate. We try to address this issue head on by arguing that shifting the architecture for citizens' individual and collective choices is as appropriate and legitimate an act for government as passing laws and regulations or creating systems of taxes and charges. Government is about citizens agreeing to tie their collective hands for collective benefit. Laws exist to protect our property and freedom, and taxes are there to pay for services societies think should be collectively provided. If supporting civic behaviour brings similar collective benefits then there appears no reason to rule it out, although other forms of policy intervention are also desirable and some checks and balances are needed on what can be done.

## How to change civic behaviour: nudge and think strategies

Understanding what motivates people and what drives their behaviour is self-evidently central to policy-making. If policy-makers are trying to change human society for the better then they are likely to have some theory of what it is that makes human beings tick. Social scientists have not yet produced a fully evidenced understanding of human behaviour, but research to date has produced at least two schools of thought that can be identified. The key issue from the point of view of policy-makers is which school to side with. In this chapter we make the argument for looking at civic behaviour through the summary ideas of nudge and think. Nudge is about giving information and social cues so as to help people do positive things for themselves and society.

9

Think argues it is possible to get citizens to think through challenging issues in innovative ways that allow for evidence, and the opinions of all, to count.

These ideas draw on different traditions of research and theory, which are explored in this chapter. The two approaches of nudge and think are different. For the decision-makers, they represent different models of how to intervene in society at large. The book by Thaler and Sunstein (Thaler and Sunstein 2008) called *Nudge: Improving Decisions about Health, Wealth and Happiness* deserves particular credit because, along with associated publications by its authors, it has done much to set out so clearly the possibilities of tackling issues of behaviour change in new ways. Nudge offers a valuable framework for changing the choice architecture of citizens in order to achieve alterations in their behaviour and attitudes, which would constitute improvements for them and for society as a whole. Nudge summarizes ideas that are current in the work of behavioural economics, which draws extensively on assumptions from psychology about heuristics and which has been applied to a range of current problems, such as understanding contributions to pension schemes. Researchers using this approach argue that citizens can be offered a choice architecture that encourages them to act in a way that achieves benefits for themselves and for their fellow citizens. This is often about the provision of information, and how it may be structured or framed to achieve effects on individual behaviour. This relatively new social-science thinking has started to influence policy-makers.

A valuable account of how nudge ideas have been taken up in practice, and how they could be taken further, is provided in a 2010 report by the Institute of Government for the UK Cabinet Office seeking to encourage policy-makers to think beyond the tools of regulation, law and financial incentives. The report contends:

> For policy-makers facing policy challenges such as crime, obesity, or environmental sustainability, behavioural approaches offer a potentially powerful new set of tools. Applying these tools can lead to low cost, low pain ways of nudging citizens – or ourselves – into new ways of acting by going with the grain of how we think and act. This is an important idea at any time, but is especially relevant in a period of fiscal constraint. (Dolan, Hallsworth, Halpern and King 2010: 7)

Nudging is emerging as an important strategy for public authorities to adopt for changing civic behaviour. The good news, according to Thaler and Sunstein, is that policy-makers may be successful in nudging citizens into civic behaviour if they take into account the cognitive architecture of choice that faces citizens and work with, rather than against, the grain of biases, hunches and heuristics. Whilst not denying the power of sticks and carrots in changing behaviour, they argue for the relevance of insights from cognitive psychology privileging the design of those interventions that recognize that citizens are boundedly rational decision-makers. The recommendation is that governments think of default options when they offer citizens choices.

An alternative strategy for transforming civic behaviour – labelled as think – emerges from the deliberative turn that has dominated democratic theory over the last couple of decades. While there are a number of different conceptions of deliberative democracy, they share a common insight: the legitimacy of politics rests on public deliberation between free and equal citizens. Deliberative theorists recognize that preferences are not independent of institutional settings. In fact, institutional settings play a role in shaping preferences. As such, decision-making procedures should not just be concerned with simply aggregating pre-existing preferences (for example, voting), but also with the nature of the processes through which they are formed. Legitimacy rests on the free flow of discussion and exchange of views in an environment of mutual respect and understanding.

Underpinning this conception of politics is a particular theory of civic behaviour that has an epistemic and moral dimension. Free and equal public deliberation has an educational effect as citizens increase their knowledge and understanding of the consequences of their actions. But the value of deliberation does not simply rest on the exchange of information. The public nature of deliberation is crucial. Because citizens are expected to justify their perspectives and preferences in public, there is a strong motivation to constrain self-interest and to consider the public good. Miller refers to the 'moralising effect of public deliberation' (Miller 1992: 61), which tends to eliminate irrational preferences based on false empirical beliefs, morally repugnant preferences which no one is willing to advance in the public arena and narrowly self-interested preferences. Citizens are given the opportunity to think differently and in so doing, deliberative theorists argue, they will witness a transformation of (often ill-informed) preferences. Deliberative democrats provide a clear account of civic behaviour: under deliberative conditions citizens' behaviour is shaped in a more civic orientation as they consider the views and perspectives of others. For many deliberative theorists, this makes deliberation (or a think strategy) particularly pertinent for including those whose voices are not often heard, and for dealing with particularly contentious public policy issues (Gutmann and Thompson 1996).

Theories of deliberative democracy are often charged with being far too utopian in their ambition: their aim appears unrealistic if it is to imbue all of politics with the virtues of mutual respect and understanding (Shapiro 2005). But more recent work has been more practical in its objectives, with democratic theorists and political scientists turning their attention to the empirical question of the conditions under which the norms and procedures of deliberation (or something close to deliberation) can be realized. There has been particular interest in forms of empowered participatory governance (Fung and Wright 2003) and democratic innovations (Smith 2009) that aim to increase and deepen citizen participation in political decision-making processes.

## A shared starting assumption: bounded rationality

Nudge and think are distinctive strategies but crucially the starting point for both is the recognition that people are boundedly rational. Citizens – those in government and those in civil society – are decision-makers constrained by the fundamental human problem of processing information, understanding a situation and determining consequences. There are limits to their cognitive capacity and the world is a complex place to understand: 'Humans are goal directed, understand their environment in realistic terms, and adjust to changing circumstances facing them. But they are not completely successful in doing so because of the inner limitations. Moreover, these cognitive limitations make a major difference in human affairs – in the affairs of individuals and in the affairs of state and nation.' (Jones 2001: 21). Decision-making is conditioned by the cognitive limitations of the human mind.

Individuals reason, but not as heroic choice-makers. When faced with a decision they do not think about every available option nor always make a great choice that is optimal to their utility, as assumed by many economists. Their cognitive inner world helps them to focus on some things and ignore others and it is driven by habits of thought, rules of thumb and emotions. Rationality is bounded by this framing role of the human mind. People will search selectively, basing that search on incomplete information and partial ignorance, but terminate it before an optimal option emerges, and will choose instead something that is good enough. This is not to say that the behaviour of agents needs to be judged as irrational. On the contrary, people are rational in the sense that behaviour is generally goal-oriented and, usually, they have reasons for what they do. It is just that rationality rests on the interaction of the cognitive structure and the context in which individuals are operating, and as a result sometimes they make poor quality decisions.

The starting point for our understanding in this area is the pioneering work of the Nobel Prize-winning Herbert Simon who produced his powerful insights over sixty years ago (Simon 1945/1997). Decision-making is conditioned by the structure of the human mind and the context in which people operate. Decision-makers rarely comprehensively perceive the environment and weigh up all options against their preferences in the context of incentives and constraints, and then efficiently choose the options that maximize these preferences. Decision-makers have to deal with the external environment and their inner world, their cognitive architecture. The inner world helps them to focus on some things and ignore others and it is driven by habits of thought, rules of thumb and emotions. Rationality is bounded by this framing role of the human mind.

A second point, strongly emphasized by Simon, is that actors gain their purpose in this complex world of information processing through sub-goal identification (Simon 1945/1997). Individuals identify with institutions or, more broadly, cultures of which they become part and internalize the aims of these social groups (Goodin 2004). More broadly, people are social animals who often look to know what the rules are in different situations and ask how it is that people are supposed to behave. Individuals search for the rules of appropriate behaviour rather than just maximize their utility (March and Olsen 1989).

Nudge and think constitute different responses to the challenge of bounded rationality. A standard assumption of much government policy-making in the past is that 'if we provide the carrots and sticks, alongside accurate information, people will weigh up the revised costs and benefits of their actions and respond accordingly' (Dolan *et al.* 2010: 8). An awareness of bounded rationality indicates that there are obvious limits to the chances of such strategies succeeding. Operating with an awareness of the implications of bounded rationality would appear to be advantageous.

So nudge tries to go with the grain of human behaviour: understand the short cuts and heuristics that people use to make decisions and then seek to bend or influence their environment – choice architecture, to use the jargon – to get behaviour that is more beneficial for society and the individual. Since individuals make decisions in the present – the here and now – nudge strategies are about creating the conditions to make better choices in the moment. A nudge strategy advocates working by understanding the way that rationality is bounded and then nudging citizens in the right direction.

In contrast, a think strategy suggests that a public agency can seek to create the right institutional framework so that an individual can overcome some aspects of their bounded rationality. If bounded rationality is heightened by lack of information and lack of attention to the viewpoints of others, then public agencies might create the conditions in which these are taken on board, in this way nudging citizens to think. This could be a fusion of our two strategies. Overall, a think strategy aims to promote free and fair deliberation between citizens. As Fearon comments, 'democratic deliberation has the capacity to lessen the problem of bounded rationality: the fact that our imaginations and calculating abilities are limited and fallible' (Fearon 1998: 49). Deliberation offers the conditions under which actors can widen their own limited and fallible perspectives by drawing on each other's knowledge, experience and capabilities. The odds of good judgements increase for two reasons: deliberation can be additively valuable in the sense that one actor is able to offer an analysis or solutions that had not occurred to others; or it can be multiplicatively valuable in that deliberation could lead to solutions that would not have occurred to the participants individually (Fearon 1998: 50).

Nudge and think have a shared starting point but present a different dynamic for change. They appeal to the different sensibilities citizens have about what is politically possible and acknowledge the extent of social change that different kinds of people think can be achieved. This chapter explores those differences before returning to the issue of whether, and how, to go about changing civic behaviour.

## Nudge: from psychological insight into intervention

Nudge strategies build on cognitive short cuts or social influences to develop an intervention which will shape civic behaviour. We briefly outline some examples of the approach below.

## Cognitive-driven interventions

Prospect theory (Kahneman and Tversky 1979; Thaler 1980) concerns the endowment effect, which suggests that when individuals are already in possession of something, they are very reluctant to lose it. Cognitively, it is more important for people to hold on to what they have (that is, to prevent loss) than to gain something extra. Experimental research backs up this theory and demonstrates that ownership matters in people's valuation of a good, with owners placing higher value on the traded good than buyers do (Kahneman, Knetsch and Thaler 1990). In public policy this translates into designing behavioural change strategies to emphasize losses rather than gains. Where people feel that they have something to lose, they may be more inclined to do something to prevent the loss occurring. For instance, smoking cessation policies that highlight years of life lost through smoking are more effective than those highlighting years gained by quitting. In a similar way, fines are likely to be a more powerful motivator for changing behaviour than rewards (Dawney and Shah 2005).

Another facet of cognitive architecture that displays less than fully rational behaviour is the use of psychological discounting (Frederick, Loewenstein and O'Donoghue 2002). This theory suggests that immediacy is a major factor in our responsiveness to offers. We place more weight on the short-term than on the long-term effects of our decisions. If people are about to gain something, they would rather do so now than later. If they have to feel pain, they would rather experience it some time in the distant future. Behavioural economists use this principle to explain why people often make imperfect economic decisions. Hyperbolic discounting occurs when we place a 'high discount rate over short horizons and a relatively low discount rate over long horizons' (Laibson 1997: 445). In other words, people overweigh short-term consumption while discounting the greater long-term gains that could be made by delaying consumption, creating outcomes that are suboptimal both from an individual and a collective perspective. It is this that makes many people reluctant to save for their retirement or inclined to ignore the long-term effects of a poor diet or exercise regime. Since we are all living longer, this psychological predisposition is one that public policies should address. Commitment mechanisms can be built into public policies to redress our propensity for short-term gratification and procrastination (O'Donoghue and Rabin 1999). One example of this, which displays promising results, is a pension savings programme built on a buy-now-pay-later principle in which employees have to commit to incremental savings with a two-year payment holiday to begin with (Thaler and Bernartzi 2004). Discounting is a feature of analysis by economists as well, but the psychological literature suggests that people discount in a less consistent and rational way than some economists, working with formally derived micro-foundations, recognize.

A closely related phenomenon is our propensity for maintaining the status quo (Samuelson and Zeckhauser 1988). Limited by time, intellectual energy and resources, the majority of people, most of the time, prefer not to change their habits unless they really have to. Research verifies that when confronted with a complex or difficult decision, and in the absence of full information about all the alternatives, individuals will often stick with their current position (Choi, Laibson, Madrian and Metrick 2003). A powerful mechanism that can be used by policy-makers is to alter the choice architecture by shifting the default position to maximize social welfare (Thaler and Sunstein 2008). Automatically enrolling citizens for pension savings programmes (Cronqvist and Thaler 2004) or on to organ donor registers (Johnson and Goldstein 2003; Abadie and Gay 2006) are instances where changing defaults appears to work well.

A further aspect of behaviour recognized by social psychologists and relevant to the design of public services is the issue of cognitive consistency. Following Festinger (Festinger 1957), psychologists suggest that people seek consistency between their beliefs and their behaviour. However, when beliefs and behaviour clash (the phenomenon of cognitive dissonance), we frequently alter beliefs instead of adjusting behaviour. One way out of this difficulty from a behaviour change perspective is to extract commitments from people (Dawney and Shah 2005). Research indicates that when people make such a commitment they feel more motivated to adjust their behaviour to back up their expressed beliefs, particularly where commitments are made in public. Making a commitment to do something can change self-image and encourage people in future decisions to seek consistency with their previous commitments. Evidence in the field of environmental behaviour suggests that extracting public promises can help to improve composting rates and water efficiency as compared to simple information provision and advertising (McKenzie-Mohr 2000). Similar findings are reported in the area of voting behaviour, with those asked beforehand to predict their likelihood of voting more likely to vote than those not asked (Greenwald, Carnot, Beach and Young 1987; see also Smith, Gerber and Orlich 2003); and in blood donation decisions, where exposing people to what is called an active decision choice (that is actively putting the choice before them) increases blood donation rates in people who are uncertain on the subject (Stutzer, Goette and Zehnder 2006).

## Interventions driven by social influences

However, individuals as conceived by psychologists do not live in isolation, and recognition of the interpersonal, community and social influences shaping behaviour will strengthen public service designs. Social psychologists and sociologists suggest a number of important influences (for a review see Cabinet Office 2004). For instance, perception of how people see each other, particularly peers, matters. In the context of promoting energy efficiency within offices, there is evidence that the technique of information disclosure between firms creates a race to the top amongst firms keen to display their green credentials (Thaler and Sunstein 2008). Similarly, the concept of social proof suggests that when confronted with an ambiguous situation, we look to other people for cues on how to behave (Cialdini 2007).

Theories of inter-group bias stress the importance of group loyalties and identifications, and experimental work indicates that strangers divided into groups can quickly form such loyalties (Tajfel, Billig, Bundy and Flament 1971) Group identities often develop, and generally speaking we are predisposed to emulate the behaviour of those with whom we identify (Tajfel and Turner 1986). Techniques that exploit these inter-group biases and loyalties have been used in policy interventions to encourage neighbourhood commitment to recycling. Such insights applied to public policy can help create policy designs that provide the opportunity for people to emulate and learn from those with whom they identify. Existing peer support and community mentoring schemes already exploit these principles. Inter-group biases can also be channelled to encourage communities to protect and steward their local environments.

A further strand of work suggests that immediate social networks, based on social norms, including reciprocity and mutuality, influence individual behaviour (House 1981). Public policy instruments such as community contracts and other forms of voluntary agreements, as well as campaigns to encourage organ donation or volunteering that emphasize reciprocity or a sense of community, make use of such principles.

## Think in practice: from democratic theory to institutional intervention

Deliberative democracy initially emerged as a highly abstract theoretical endeavour: the province of academic theorists. Since the late 1990s, however, an increasing number of political scientists and democratic theorists have begun to pay attention to the institutional conditions that can foster deliberation. It is this literature – particularly recent work on democratic innovations that aims to increase and deepen citizen participation in political decision-making (Fung 2003a; Smith 2009) – that can inform think strategies. Radically different designs have the potential to promote deliberation. One of the most commonly celebrated is participatory budgeting which emerged in Porto Alegre (Brazil) in the late 1980s, but the influence of which has been felt across Latin America, into Europe and beyond (Cabannes 2004). Similarly, a great deal of attention has been focused on mini-publics such as citizens' juries and deliberative polling, which ensure inclusiveness by aiming to engage a random sample of citizens. Recently the impressive Citizens' Assemblies on Electoral Reform in British Columbia and Ontario have expanded the imagination as to how mini-publics might be employed (Warren and Pearce 2008). And, with developments in information and communications technology (ICT), there is now growing academic and practitioner interest in the potential of, for example, online discussion forums, which in principle overcome barriers to participation associated with time and scale.

While the methods of engagement differ, these innovations in citizen participation often share similar institutional characteristics that motivate a civic orientation. First, they carefully construct safe havens in which deliberation is enabled: in other words, there is a recognition that the norms and procedures of deliberation need to be nurtured and do not necessarily emerge naturally. Second, part of the motivation to participate is that citizens have a meaningful influence on significant political decisions. The unwillingness of governments to create these conditions – in particular access to influence – means that the rhetoric of deliberation and citizen engagement is undermined in practice.

The evidence from studies of democratic innovations indicates that ordinary citizens are willing and able to deliberate on controversial public issues when such interventions are carefully constructed. Institutional design is crucial in altering behaviour: bringing citizens together from diverse backgrounds (often mobilizing participants from politically marginalized social groups) and constructing an environment in which contentious issues can be debated (Smith 2009).

## Nudging and thinking compared

The starting assumption for nudge and think strategies may be the same but their responses to this challenge are dissimilar. To help clarify these differences, we set them out in Table 1.1, with the elements of each approach summarized in the two columns. This is designed to be a helpful simplification of the complexity of the two approaches.

The first difference is in the underlying view of human behaviour. Nudgers tend to assume that individuals are happy to fall back on past lines of thought and behaviour unless they are encouraged to do something different. The options for change centre on reminders and cues that accept where the individual is and then put in place a choice environment whereby society might gain from the realization of these preferences. The nudge strategy plays to the role of the state as educator and the role of the policy-maker as paternalistic expert, steering citizens down paths that are more beneficial to them and society at large. Once these are known, the designer of public policy can use these to good effect so that the result is hardly noticed by the individual. The nudge strategy accepts citizens as they are, and tries to divert them down new paths to make better decisions.

**Table 1.1**  Nudge and think compared

|  | *Nudge* | *Think* |
|---|---|---|
| View of subjects | Cognitive misers, users of shortcuts, prone to flawed sometimes befuddled thinking | Reasonable, knowledge hungry and capable of collective reflection |
| Costs to the individual | Low but repeated | High but only intermittently |
| Primary unit of analysis | The individual | The group |
| Change process | Cost-benefit led shift in choice environment | Value led outline of new shared policy platform |
| Civic conception | Increasing the attractiveness of positive-sum action | Addressing the general interest |
| Role of the state | Customize messages, expert and teacher | Create new institutional spaces to support citizen-led investigation, respond to citizens |

The think strategy has a different account of what makes humans tick. It assumes that the individual can step away from their day-to-day experience, throw off their blinkers and reflect on the wide range of policy choices and dilemmas. People can be knowledge hungry, learn to process new information and demands and reach new heights of reflection and judgement. The institutional setting and organization of the think has to be right, but if it is then citizens can extend their knowledge and understanding of issues and work together to find solutions.

The think strategy would appear then to be more demanding than the nudge strategy in the effort required by the individual to engage. Nudge relies on the impact of any intervention being low cost. In fact, it can only work through being low cost or else the individual would not cooperate. In contrast, in order to get going, the deliberative experience requires the incurring of some considerable costs. There needs to be some investment in acquiring information and then in debating with others, often in a particular context, away from the individual's normal environment. These costs have policy implications so they need to be seen alongside the benefit. The costs are partly a function of the unit of analysis. While both can be individually and collectively achieved, nudge is about affecting individual choices, just as in classical economics, though of course if the nudge is done in concert with others it stands more chance of success. Deliberation by definition cannot happen alone in spite of the powerful role that individuals play in the process.

How does change come about? For both strategies, change is achieved by altering how the individual sees the attractiveness of a different course or action. The nudge strategy seeks to improve the messages that citizens receive and the opportunities they have to participate so they see the costs in different, more congenial, ways. For the deliberative democrat, the change is about tapping into and giving life to values that are discovered and brought out through debate and reflection. Once these values are uppermost, the costs and benefits to the individual will look different and the motivation to make sacrifices to achieve them will alter. This links to the civic conception implied by each approach. The nudger does not think that the individual is entirely selfish – there is a civic conception in the nudge scheme. But the civic is limited to small acts, which might amount to a bigger societal change. The deliberative democrat would not be happy unless the general interest has been considered. Civic behaviour in deliberative forums is understood in these terms.

Finally, these two approaches differ as to the expected state action. For the nudger the role of state is about getting the messages right and giving low-level incentives and costs to get to the desired kind of behaviour, although it may require frequent and repeated application to be effective. The role of the policy-maker is as expert, someone who is able to say what is the best course of action and who is smart enough to design interventions that achieve these goals. These actions may be quite modest, even though they require a lot of thought, and they usually involve the modification of a routine or procedure. In contrast, for the think strategy to be successful, the policy-maker needs to be open-minded and willing to act as an organizer of citizen-driven investigation. Crucially, the state needs not only to provide institutions that can help citizens deliberate: if the strategy is to be sustainable, it has to follow up on the recommendations that emerge, otherwise participants are likely to be disempowered and further disengaged from the political process.

## Should public authorities change civic behaviour?

So far in this introduction we have assumed that the involvement of citizens in tackling social and economic problems is desirable. But why assume that and why consider it appropriate to design policy to stimulate civic behaviour? Our starting point is that government on its own will find it hard to address some of the common challenges of society because no matter how much money it throws at an issue or how many regulations it passes, many problems will not go away. In a period of fiscal austerity the spending option may no longer be easily available so governments have to rely even more than before on citizens helping themselves and others. It is also the case that governments in many modern industrial societies can no longer rely on deference and obedience to messages from a benevolent centre, as they did before. Citizens will question the authority of government or simply ignore it.

One response is to involve citizens directly in public policy, so as to get their consent in such a way that they own the policies, and as a result change their behaviour in an intended direction. Another is to argue that policy-makers need to go with the grain of the way individuals make decisions. They should design solutions that encourage civic behaviour rather than act against it or crowd it out. Moreover, government policy could be improved by involving the citizens in such a way that they help public authorities adjust the implementation of public policies to reflect the particular circumstances and problems of a policy sector and locale or neighbourhood. In this way, as Braybrooke and Lindblom argue, government can become more intelligent if it is guided by responding to information, in this case from the citizens (Braybrooke and Lindblom 1963). The logic of this argument is that if governments are going to be successful in a more challenging age, they need to use different kinds of instrument, ones that are smart and nimble, that are guided by the way that citizens are, and are driven by the active contribution of citizens (John 2011). The blunt instruments of financial allocation and regulation will fail or be only partly successful. The ways that governments communicate with citizens and involve them will have to be smarter and more effective.

But even if there are gains to be yielded from the kinds of policies we describe here, should government still back off because it should not interfere with individual freedom and choice? After all, it is often argued that the whole idea of representative democracy is that citizens elect governments to get on with the job of government, the media and public opinion keep them in check between elections, and the threat of being up for re-election keeps them on their toes to manage policies effectively. In subsequent elections, citizens can re-elect a government to carry on managing affairs in the same way or elect another government to do things differently. With governments in charge, the job of the bureaucracy, local government and other agencies is to do the best job of administering public services on behalf of the citizen in as efficient and cost-effective a way as possible. Does it not appear inappropriate for government to expect the citizens to contribute their time to shaping services and even to produce some of the outcomes themselves, either directly through co-producing services, or indirectly by altering their behaviour so that they, and other citizens, get a public benefit? Moreover, the public might expect a right to keep their private lives private from the state, to be free from interfering public agencies that wish to change their behaviour. If somebody wants to have an unhealthy lifestyle, they should be allowed to lead it. They are entitled to elect a government and to pay taxes for a health service to pick up the pieces.

When is it right for the state to intervene in issues of behaviour? Assessing the morality of seeking to steer people's choices in certain directions is, of course, not a new dilemma for policy-makers, and issues of whether it is right to intervene apply equally well to the use of standard tools such as law-making, regulation or taxation. What makes the issue more challenging in the case of nudging is that standard forms of intervention are more open and explicit about their intentions. (Although we can ask how much people really understand about the details of regulations and taxation. And we know also that policy tools of all types can be made less visible to reduce public resistance.) The tenor of nudging can be 'we the government know better what is good for you than you do and we have found a sneaky way of getting you to make the right choice'.

This problem becomes more acute when considering some of the techniques that governments can use to change behaviour. With the insights of behavioural economics as a guide, it can appear that public agencies are using the dark arts of manipulation to alter civic behaviour to get to good ends for society. In this sense a think strategy trumps nudge on the grounds of transparency. But even think can invite the same attack. If society accepts that governments should involve citizens in decisions about the delivery of services, is not this a form of compulsion or an invitation to a self-selected minority to make decisions for the rest of society? Democratic governments, which are supposed to be responsive and to respect individual freedoms, may feel uncomfortable at taking such a direct control over the private lives of many citizens without their active consent. In the rest of the book, naturally we answer this question in the negative, largely because citizens expect governments to get on with the job of making effective policies and only want to blame them when things go seriously wrong. But it is clear that behaviour change is a sensitive area, where extra attention to the democratic principles of transparency and responsiveness should guide policy-makers in the design of these interventions, even more so than other policies. If not, these interventions risk being seen as illegitimate and they will become ineffective as a result. Interventions designed to foster behavioural change need to be as public as possible, with as much support from the public as is feasible. One line of defence for nudge strategies promoted by Thaler and Sunstein (Thaler and Sunstein 2008), and appearing under the label of libertarian paternalism, is that at least the choice does remain with the citizen – it is just the architecture of choice that is altered to support what are judged by democratic governments to be beneficial outcomes.

Another important point is that our current choice architecture is neither natural nor morally neutral – in fact, in many ways it is pernicious and undermines civic behaviour. Individuals make decisions in the light of social mores and norms influenced by the market, commercial advertising, peer pressure, ignorance and habit. Choice architectures are constantly evolving through strategic action on the part of different actors and the unintentional impact of everyday activities. So policy-makers, by seeking to steer the choice architecture, are just one more framer of choice for the citizen. But unlike other influencers they are at least authorized through the democratic process to promote the common good. And one way to do this is to encourage civic behaviour.

If the qualms about intervention can be met, there remains, of course, the issue of competence. Can we trust governments to make the right choices for us? Prabhakar argues:

Behavioural economics assumes that government knows best. But often this may not be the case. For good reason, government might find it difficult to unpick the different parts of a policy problem ... government might lack proper evidence to guide its decisions. Government might only know the right nudges in a limited number of areas where there is plenty of evidence. (Prabhakar 2010)

Policy-makers after all face the same challenge of bounded rationality as citizens in civil society. In a different way, think strategists have been challenged because of their tendency to assume they know what is best for people (Stoker 2006). People are supposed to choose between options not on the basis of self-interest but rather on the basis of a judgement about which of the options will advance the group's agenda. And whether they make the right choice or not depends in large part on whether the participants follow the procedures and norms of deliberation (Fung and Wright 2003). There is a danger that in trying to design out difficulties, think strategists are fostering forms of governance that in practice can become rigid and deeply constrained and not all that participatory, because only what are considered acceptable behaviours and reasonable demands are allowed to find their place in its processes and outputs. In their different ways, both think and nudge may be perceived as authoritarian if they are not introduced to the reference points of the citizens with a great deal of sensitivity, so that the individual is ultimately in control of his or her fate, even if governments play a role in structuring the information to the citizen and affecting the institutional context in which action and debate takes place.

These arguments are a useful qualification to overenthusiasm about changing civic behaviour but are not convincing enough to suggest governments should abandon the project. When government taxes and regulates citizens how does government know it is doing the best thing? The answer in all cases is surely that the key issue is a judgement for which, in a democratic society, citizens can hold government to account at some point. Moreover our existing choice architecture is a construction of the decisions (or non-decisions) of actors, institutions and practices that (explicitly or implicitly) promote non-civic behaviour. Looked at in this way it would be remiss for policy-makers to neglect the options for changing civic behaviour.

Of course, nudge versus think is not the only take on what governments can do to encourage civic-minded behaviour. The traditional tools in the armoury of governments – regulatory and economic instruments – can and are used to shape civic actions. Tax incentives can provide a fiscal incentive to reduce carbon usage, or rewards can be offered for good behaviour on housing estates. The law can be used to compel people to be civic, such as those laws aimed at stopping dog-fouling on footpaths and in parks. But the attraction of nudge and think is that they are not about government commands, but about creating the conditions for better citizen choice.

## Conclusion

In this chapter, we have reviewed the intellectual origins and implications of our two theoretical positions, summarized as nudge and think. These terms are, of course, simplifications of complex literatures and research programmes that have many manifestations, and range across different kinds of motivations and causes of human behaviour. But we hope we have conveyed an important distinction between ways of thinking about behaviour change, with nudge being more concerned to provide cues to individuals to do better for society; and with think strategies being more interested in presenting individuals with opportunities to debate the key issues so they gain the resources and motivation to act. And, in many ways, think may be seen as a more positive alternative to nudge, and one that is more open and respectful of the individual. It is more transparent, too. In practice, these approaches are closer together than they might at first seem. Both acknowledge the limits to individual change and the lack of capacity individuals have in their everyday lives and decision-making for weighing up all the options that are open to them – the constraints of bounded rationality. Both these perspectives offer alternatives to policy-makers that are different from the top-down and commanding tools of the state that have been used so much in recent years; moreover, they are both capable of looking at public policy in a more citizen-centred way, a form of policy-making that is increasingly fashionable across the world. At the same time, because these interventions are new, they have attracted the suspicion of critics who see them as paternalistic and undemocratic – even think because of its reliance on selected groups of citizens. We hope to counter such concerns.

As we shall show later in the book, most of these softer interventions in practice are often some combination of nudge and think – for example, democratic innovations can be understood as the active design of structures that nudge citizens towards thinking. In this way, we offer a reconstruction of nudge that uses elements of think to make it more transparent, effective and legitimate.

Most of all, these new tools of government need more testing and evaluation. And this is just what we do in the remaining chapters of this book. But before that – in the next chapter – we consider the best way to acquire robust knowledge about what works.

# 2

# Testing

This book aims to identify the best strategies that policy-makers could adopt to encourage citizens to carry out collectively beneficial acts. Policy-makers need to know whether the nudge and think measures they introduce can achieve their desired effects or not. They require warrantable knowledge that tells them that if they do X then Y happens. They need to calculate how much of an impact a unit of a policy (X) has on a unit of an outcome (Y). They want to know how much an intervention costs in relation to the costs and benefits of other policy choices. In other words, they need a way of acquiring knowledge that apprises them of the causal relationships in the world, and informs them about just how much government and public agencies can influence those relationships in comparison with other ways of using their capacity and resources.

The argument that policy should be based on sound research seems obvious, but governments and public agencies often intervene without good evidence of whether the measures they introduce do in fact work: 'both decision makers and social scientists are content to rely on seat-of-the-pants intuitions rather than conduct the sorts of tests that could contribute to knowledge' (Green and Gerber 2003: 105). Getting it right might be the result of luck rather than foresight. Policy-makers can get lucky, of course; but it is likely also that they are not serendipitous and there will not be a positive outcome resulting from an intervention – or even a negative one. To illustrate this point, Torgerson and Torgerson give examples of practices that were widely used in healthcare and believed to be effective until randomized controlled trials showed many years later that they did not work (Torgerson and Torgerson 2008: 4–7). In the 1940s and 1950s, oxygen was routinely given to premature babies after birth, and it was only after a randomized controlled trial found that oxygen led to significant increases in blindness that the practice was stopped. In crime policy, the programme called Scared Straight, which got young people to meet convicted criminals so as to shock them into not offending, was shown by a series of trials to have had the opposite effect to what was intended, actually increasing the risk of offending by juveniles (Petrosino, Turpin-Petrosino and Buehler 2003).

As a result of making policy based on poor evaluations, public resources have been wasted. Money could be spent on other items of benefit rather than on useless interventions or taxes could be lowered. Null or negative results can even discredit the whole approach of involving citizens in public policy and can be used as evidence to say that governments should not interfere with civil society.

So what can be done about poorly evidenced public policies? One answer is to look for existing evidence. There are many sources that governments and other agencies can use when they select strategies to try to affect civic behaviour – or any other outcome. They could trust the views they get from practitioners; make use of expert testimonies; commission reviews of the international experience; rely on the personal experience of civil servants and ministers. Each of these sources has some value, but they should not be relied upon alone and can lead to the poor policies described above. Better are the many techniques in social science, such as case studies, analyses of the statistical evidence and multi-method evaluations of existing policies. This is because the approach to collecting evidence is systematic, where great care is taken to try to relate an intervention to an outcome and to rule out other factors that might have also caused it.

Whilst not wishing governments to cast aside these existing sources of evidence (both informal and social scientific), the argument we present in this chapter is that experiments – especially randomized controlled trials – offer a much more valid and robust standard of evidence than any other method policy-makers have available. In fact, policy-makers should seek to use, as far as possible, the evidence from randomized controlled trials for their decisions on matters of public policy. At the moment, the commissioning and use of trials are all too rare.

To support this view, we offer an outline of the method of the randomized controlled trial and its qualitative equivalent, the design experiment. We argue that these different kinds of experiments have the capacity to provide robust evaluations of interventions designed to change civic behaviour. The chapter contains an explanation of why experimental methods have tended to be neglected, and highlights some of the pitfalls of the approach and how they may be overcome. We conclude that there is considerable untapped potential in randomized controlled trials, both for social scientists and policy-makers.

## Standards of proof

It is often frustrating for policy-makers to hear advice from social scientists. Quite often social scientists will say they do not know what works, or perhaps that the evidence is strong, but they do not know what the impact will be across the whole country. Or sometimes the opposite happens. A study is carried out that indicates that the government's policy works, but afterwards social scientists find the early evaluation was over-optimistic and produced some invalid inferences that did not apply later or elsewhere. These problems emerge from the challenge of making predictions and claims about the social world. The complexity of society creates a large number of interactions that vary from place to place. This makes it difficult to produce generalizations that hold over space, and over time, too (Pawson and Tilly 1997). Then there is the problem of knowing whether the evidence actually shows what it purports to show, which is about the limits of the instruments researchers have to observe the world.

The problem of making a generalization in social sciences comes down to the problem of validity, which is about the extent to which the research allows an inference to be made that there is the hypothesized causal effect (see Table 2.1).

**Table 2.1** Validity

| |
|---|
| *General Validity:* <br> The extent to which it is possible to make inferences from a piece of research |
| *External Validity:* <br> The extent to which the inference from a piece of research can be generalized to other contexts from where or when the research took place |
| *Internal Validity:* <br> Whether the research explains what has happened - the extent to which it is possible to conclude that there is a hypothesized relationship between cause and effect |

The first issue with validity is external – whether it is possible to generalize from the intervention to other places and times. The problem occurs because of the difficulty of reproducing the same conditions under which the original intervention or pilot was monitored – the complexity problem again. The second issue with validity concerns whether the instruments we have to hand validly observe the causal relations that are hypothesized to be happening in the real world – internal validity. One reason for weak internal validity is that the instruments do not always measure what happens. For example, views about the success of a policy might be drawn from survey responses of those who were involved with or who had participated in the intervention. But because those responding to the survey have a stake in the success of the policy, they may over-report the good aspects of the intervention and under-report the negative side. This happens – not from any willingness to deceive – but because the person responding has a perception of the policy from being involved in it, and that comes out in the survey response.

There is a further problem. It may be the case that the method does not offer a counterfactual as to what would have happened had the policy not been introduced. This is because the act of introducing the policy and measuring it may select favourable locations or create special conditions that affect its success but which would not apply when it is rolled out more generally across the country. This is similar to the survey response problem. Moreover, people who are more likely to achieve a desirable set of outcomes select into, i.e. choose to be become involved in, the programme to be evaluated, so, for example, pilots of employment schemes may end up training people who find it easy to get a job anyway so the result is more successful than it would be if the scheme were rolled out nationally. Or the areas that become selected into the research are those that are most ahead of the others in the first place or have more potential to improve. Even survey respondents may select into responding, with those more favourably disposed more likely to fill out a questionnaire, just as the students who fill out course evaluations are likely to be those who stayed until the end of the course, while those who were discontented dropped out long before. Moreover, the act of researching and evaluating may create what is called a Hawthorne effect (see Table 2.2), whereby those people affected by an intervention improve their outcomes because they are in the pilot. Participants do better because they feel more committed and enthusiastic when someone is observing them, as well as worrying about being watched and monitored.

**Table 2.2** The Hawthorne effect

| The effect of the research on the outcome itself because research subjects respond to the interest being shown in them and change their behaviour accordingly. This may lead to the inference that an intervention has worked when it has not. |
| --- |

These are examples of false positives, where the research shows something works but in fact it does not, and it is common to find evaluations of policy saying that an intervention has succeeded when it is based on observational evidence. Bias can work the opposite way, too. An intervention might show no impact, but that could be because factors independent of the intervention had caused every area or all people to reduce their performance. Simply observing the change in outcomes of those who had the intervention might lead the researcher to infer a false negative. What is needed is a counterfactual, which tells the researcher what would have happened in the absence of the intervention.

## The advantages of comparison

In order to produce a counterfactual, most methods of evaluation build-in comparison as a key part of their methodology. Drawing on the work of J.S. Mill, many scholars regard comparison as the key feature of social science, assisting in their understanding of the impact of institutions, cultures and policy choices, by attempting to compare what happens with, or without, the occurrence of some hypothesized factor (Przeworski and Teune 1970). In evaluation research, it is possible to compare people, groups or areas that were the subject of a policy intervention with others that were not, or perhaps with those who experienced the intervention later, or in a different or more systematic way. This evaluation can be achieved by using statistics to measure the impact over all cases, or over a sample, so that the average effect is observed, connecting variations in the factors that affect an outcome with variations in the outcome itself. Or else case studies can compare carefully selected areas and seek to understand why contrasting and similar areas produce outcomes. It is possible to be ingenious with the research design to improve the leverage, such as by looking at small variations within a case (King, Keohane and Verba et al 1994; Gerring 2006). It can be instructive to observe change over time, particularly if it is possible to rule out other explanations for the change. For example, some evaluation research makes inferences from what are called interrupted time series, where the impact of an intervention over time is compared to a comparison group that did not receive the intervention (see Shadish, Cook and Campbell 2002). Even though these observational studies have merit, they cannot rule out the possibility that the outcomes they compare may have been caused by things other than the intervention. This may be because the comparison group was different in some way, perhaps as a result of not being selected to have the intervention, or being selected to have it in different ways, or simply because something unexpected happened to one or both groups.

## The power of randomization

It should be clear where the argument in this chapter is headed. The best way to compare individuals, groups or areas that have had or have not had the intervention is to make a random allocation. Because the differences between the groups have been removed by randomization and, when the sample size is large enough, the only other factors that might cause a difference in outcomes – outside chance – is the intervention itself.

A diagram best represents how a randomized controlled trial works (see Figure 2.1). There are three stages that in many respects resemble what researchers do in a standard research design, but there are important modifications in the randomized controlled trial. The first is the selection of a population of interest that should relate to the research question and be the units the policy-maker or researcher is interested in. The second is unique to randomized controlled trials and involves randomization of the population into treatment (intervention) and control groups. The random allocation ensures that the membership of the treatment and control groups is very similar in all respects. Then – third – the outcome is measured after the intervention. The researchers can compare and contrast the measured outcomes across the groups and be safe in the knowledge that any differences in observed outcomes between the groups can reasonably be attributed to the intervention rather than to any other cause. As with other comparisons, it is possible to use inferential statistics to find out whether the differences between the groups have occurred simply by chance. A well-designed randomized controlled trial can provide a convincing estimate of the effect of an intervention, revealing how much effort or amount of resources it takes to produce a certain level of outcome.

There are variations on the basic design, such as having more than one treatment group. There are different kinds of randomizations, such as those that come from a gradual implementation of a policy (the stepped wedged design). It may also be possible to measure outcomes both before and after the intervention. There are other desirable features of many experiments, for example that they should measure real outcomes, such as votes, rather than observations or survey responses. But the basic features of the trial remain the same with randomization at its core.

**Figure 2.1**  An experimental study design

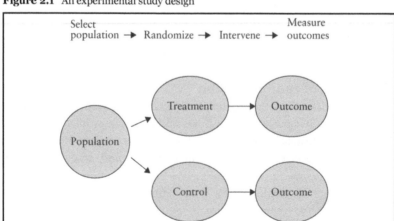

## An example: Get Out the Vote

An example helps think through the power of the method. Voting is the subject of Chapter 5, so this example is also a preparation for what we report there. The experiment we describe here aims to find out whether an intervention in the form of a Get Out the Vote campaign, such as a door-knocking campaign, can increase the propensity of voters to turn out at an election. It is impossible to know this simply from surveys that ask people whether they have been canvassed and whether they have voted because of the inaccuracy of people's memories of voting and of receiving campaign information. In addition, it is possible that the people who are known to be more willing to vote are more likely be canvassed, as well as more likely to respond to the survey. This combination might just produce a correlation between canvass and vote rather than showing that the canvass had an effect. By contrast, an experiment with a simulated Get Out the Vote campaign can find out whether canvassing works by randomly allocating voters into two groups and then canvassing only one group. In this way there is a randomized population and a measurement of the outcome in the form of actual votes, checked from electoral registers after the election. Comparing the number of people voting in the treatment group and the number voting in the control group allows us to estimate the effect of the treatment. If the number voting in the treatment groups exceeds the control group by more than might be expected by chance, then canvassing has had an effect, and this can be calculated by the percentage point difference in voting.

## Randomized controlled trials as the gold standard

Social scientists, health professionals and government researchers refer to randomized controlled trial as the gold standard (Cabinet Office 2003). This is because trials produce a more warrantable form of knowledge than other methods. They are better than other kinds of evaluation because they are able to offer a genuine counterfactual of what would have happened without the intervention. For this reason, the trial has become the main source of knowledge acquisition about the impact of drugs in the medical field, and is regarded as a superior form of evaluation for policies on education and crime (see Torgerson and Torgerson 2008).

If an experiment is well designed and conducted effectively, researchers and policy-makers are able to infer whether there is a causal impact from the intervention or not. If the result is replicated again in a several trials, they are in an even stronger position to make causal inferences (Torgerson and

Torgerson 2008). Researchers are at pains to stress that they do not want to advocate randomized controlled trials as the only form of policy evaluation. There are some drawbacks, as with all methods, and we will discuss these later in the chapter. Other methods can be very useful for different things, such as determining stakeholder perceptions of a policy, which can be ascertained from a survey, or establishing whether the income of a particular group went up or not during the period of an intervention. Our message in this chapter is that these methods are not ideal for determining the impact of a particular intervention as distinct from other influential factors affecting the outcome. Experimental research provides a more secure foundation for causal inference in these contexts.

We make an argument for field experiments, which take place in the real world. Druckman *et al.* argue that field experiments 'take advantage of *naturally occurring* political contexts while simultaneously leveraging the inferential benefits of random assignment. Because of their "realistic" foundations, field experiments can be especially relevant to policymakers' (Druckman, Green, Kuklinski and Lupia 2006: 627; italics in the original). As Green and Gerber point out, there are more opportunities created to make the case for experiments in real policy settings than many social scientists have recognized (Green and Gerber 2003). Advocates of field experiments argue that the weight given to a body of research should be in proportion to the uncertainty associated with its bias (see also Gerber, Green and Kaplan 2004). In other words, researchers need to observe the maxim: 'The more dubious the leap from research findings to a proposed application, the less weight should be accorded to the findings' (Green and Gerber 2003: 100). On this basis, political scientists should attach far less value to observational research. Moreover, laboratory work may be vulnerable to challenge because of the contrived settings in which it is conducted.

The implementation of new programmes, the diversity created through decentralized structures and even financial constraints that encourage piloting rather than full-throttle roll-out provide a context in which experimentation can come to the fore. Experimenters need to work closely with policy-makers and social actors in order to both create the opportunities for field experiments and also achieve the mantle of relevance by helping in the search for solutions to tractable research and policy questions. Green and Gerber provide a rallying cry for experimenters to step forward and engage with policy-makers arguing that:

through systematic intrusion into the world, experimentation may encourage political scientists to rethink the relationship between political science and society. By continual interaction with those who are sceptical of social science, these intrusions force political scientists to ask whether decades of investigation have produced anything of demonstrable practical value. This question looms large over the future development of the discipline. If scholars can demonstrate the practical benefits of science, those who have the discretion and resources to effect change will learn to seize opportunities to acquire knowledge. (Green and Gerber 2003: 110)

The relationship between field experiments and policy could be symbiotic. Experiments can offer significant advances in knowledge creation and can make social science relevant. According to Roth, one of the key uses of experiments is to enable academics to engage with the policy process (Roth 1995: 22). This is partly because policy-makers can identify the robust evidence produced by experiments and can relate to the headline results, whereas other kinds of research are often inconclusive (for example, case studies) or are hard to penetrate (such as the technical language of panel regression analysis).

## Using the experimental method

Experiments are not a panacea for evaluating public policy interventions. They are much better than any competitor so they should be adopted at any opportunity. But, as with any method, they need to be adopted carefully and researchers should not claim more than can be inferred from the results. Because of this, as Shadish, Cook and Campbell argue, experimenters have largely abandoned earlier claims to produce unvarnished, superior knowledge in favour of a more nuanced claim about producing better knowledge (Shadish *et al.* 2002: 29–31). The experiment is a profoundly human endeavour, affected by all the same human foibles as any other human enterprise, though with well-developed procedures for partial control of some of the limitations that have been identified to date (Shadish *et al.* 2002: 30). Experiments are not to be put on a pedestal but they are a cornerstone scientific method and are rightly becoming a tool that is increasingly adopted by political scientists because of their unrivalled capacity to establish causal inferences. Their limits should not be seen as undermining this research method, but as the product of mature reflection, which encourages a more sensitive application of randomized controlled trials. After all, if too much is claimed from trials, policy-makers are bound to become disappointed. Moreover, there are ways to overcome these problems without great difficulty.

The first limitation is that experiments tend to be carried out in particular localities rather than as a nationwide trial, usually because of the complexity of arranging interventions (see below). These local results mean it is sometimes hard to generalize from localized experiments to other parts of the country, or from country to country. In the language of methodology, experiments are strong in internal validity but weak in external validity (see Table 2.1 above). The response of the experimenter is to argue that the knowledge base is improved by the accumulation of evidence. In this way, when trials are repeated in several contexts, and at different times, with different populations and different delivery partners, knowledge is accumulated. When the same basic results keep appearing, we know for certain that there is a robust relationship. Meta analysis – the analysis of many trials in one data analysis – can help to get a sense of what is the general relationship.

A related issue is that experiments tend to isolate those aspects of an intervention that are capable of being randomized and are less good at evaluating the intervention as a whole. Some aspects of an intervention can be randomized more easily than others and are selected for the evaluation, which means the experiment does not fully evaluate what government is doing in its policy intervention, for example, or it encourages government to select policies in easily randomized units rather than in other more useful ways which are not susceptible to trials. A new policy may take time to work, whereas the experimenter might be tempted to pull out the short-term effects (though this problem is not unique to randomized controlled trials). The challenge once again is to accumulate knowledge about different aspects of an intervention and to match them with other kinds of evidence.

Experimenters need to be careful to address a number of technical issues when implementing experiments. In particular, randomization may be hard to achieve in practice. It is possible to have an unbalanced randomization purely from random error so that the two groups do not start from the same point. One solution is to control this in a regression model where covariates isolate the effects on the outcomes as well as the intervention. The other solution is to do checks on the randomization and to repeat the randomization in the rare case that the groups end up unequal (experimenters differ on the merits of this). In general, this is a minor problem.

Another problem is that there may also be differential selection into the treatment and control groups, particularly if participants are invited into these groups or have a chance to drop out. The treatment itself may either encourage participants to drop out if they do not want to take part in it, or being in the control group might lead to disappointment followed by attrition. Differential selection also occurs if it is not possible to treat all the treatment group, as in a classic Get Out the Vote campaign described above, where not everyone will be in to answer their door to the campaign team. As in the case of breaches to randomization, this means that the groups are not the same, because the treatment group divides up into people who were contacted and people who were not contacted. But, as with randomization, it is possible to allow for how people select into the treatment and still produce a valid estimate of the treatment. Again, this is not usually a major problem, but these statistical procedures tend to detract from the purity of the experimental method.

One key issue – and this relates to some of the experiments described in this book – is that the experiment may be compromised by the practitioners, even those with the best of intentions. It is possible that the treatment may not be administered properly or that the agency involved may begin another intervention at the same time (Cotterill and Richardson 2010). More generally, as we discuss below, it is difficult to carry out experiments in the field as they are often 'bedevilled by practical problems of implementation' (Jowell 2003: 17). Lack of training of the staff involved in delivering the intervention may create problems. Decisions made in the heat of the moment may prove problematic to the experiment. For example, researchers in a study of deliberation which sought to contrast a decision mode driven by consensus with a decision mode based on voting found that pressures of time moved the consensus group towards the voting style of decision-making, with the result that the comparison was less easy to sustain (Setälä, Grönlund and Herne 2007). Greenberg, Linkz and Mandell review the long history in the United States of experimental trials in the social policy field, and provide examples of where experiments have had to be abandoned or modified because of administrative and other problems (Greenberg, Linkz and Mandell 2003).

Because of this it is tempting to try to experiment without government agencies randomizing what they do, but to mimic these kinds of contact by having the researcher carry out the intervention instead, for example by creating a canvass group, or by carrying out feedback. The problem here is that the experiment lacks the force of a government intervention so the effects may be less than if the government agency was involved (though it may have the advantage that the citizens might trust a non-governmental body more than tarnished central or local government). Where researchers have to recreate the environment of policy-makers, the results may not read across from the experiment to the real world of policy implementation.

Finally, experimental research can face a number of ethical challenges. A common but misplaced criticism is that if we think an intervention might work, how can experimenters justify only the treatment group receiving that benefit? The answer, of course, is that we do not know that a benefit will accrue to the treatment group and hence the need for the experiment. As in other forms of research, a version of the harm principle could be used to judge the conduct of the experimenters in their work so that experiments could be considered ethical unless they knowingly cause harm to others. Some experiments may involve misleading participants and here if such deception cannot be avoided the best approach is to get the informed consent of those involved in the trial and debrief them afterwards. Overall, the ethical objections to experiments do not stand up to much scrutiny, especially in the civic behaviour field where there are a few negative effects of an intervention.

Overall, randomized controlled trials are the best way to find out whether an intervention worked or not, and to draw lessons about how – in our case – government may best stimulate civic behaviour. They are not without limitations, but many of the problems they face are well known and there exist some well-understood and recognized ways to overcome them.

## Design experiments

Sometimes it is not possible to carry out a trial because it is hard to randomize a population or there is not enough known about an intervention to design an effective trial. This suggests the need for an intermediate method, which can pilot the intervention and pave the way for a randomized controlled trial. What is sometimes called for is some sort of compromise to be struck between knowing everything and knowing something. Torgerson and Torgerson refer to the value of pragmatic trials (Torgerson and Torgerson 2008) and Stoker and John argue for the development of design experiments as a precursor to full-blown field experiments (Stoker and John 2009). They argue that design experiments also seek to manipulate the external world, but in a way that is different from the generalized causal inference of mainstream experimental evaluations, such as randomized controlled trials. The design experiment may be thought of as a qualitative experiment, which focuses on the design of an intervention as the thing to get right. The experimental aspect of the method manipulates an intervention and observes it over an extended time period, usually in one location, until acceptable results emerge. This is a bit like the interrupted time series discussed earlier, where the researcher observes changes as a result of an intervention. In the design version, the experiment progresses through a series of design-redesign cycles. There is feedback to the core decision-makers and to front-line bureaucrats as a policy unfolds so that the design of the policy is adjusted to work in a particular context (Stoker and John 2009: 356). Once an acceptable version of the intervention is established it may provide the starting point for a broader randomized controlled trial test of a policy.

Design experiments offer social scientists and public managers a new way of researching public policy innovations, providing insights about what works and supplying timely information to decision-makers as an intervention develops. The method draws on the experimental tradition in social science and public policy, which conceives of a policy or an intervention as a treatment, whose impact can be compared with that of a randomly allocated control group. In an analogous fashion, design experiments manipulate the external world, but in a way that is different from large-scale experimental evaluations, such as randomized controlled trials, which aim to make generalized causal inferences. The design experiment focuses on the design of an intervention as the core research problem. The methodology claims to provide an evidence base that shows how an intervention can work in its early stages, when the intervention is being developed; in this way, it may provide a staging post for a broader and more generalizable test of a policy. Trialists find it hard to conclude whether a repetition of the experiment in an alternative setting would replicate the results. The design experiment sidesteps these issues by avoiding generalized claims about causal validity. The method aims to provide detailed information about the case and its context, so that the observer gradually establishes the causal processes at work.

Design experiments need to be carried out at the outset of an intervention. The focus is on understanding and applying innovative techniques in teaching and learning. They aim for the engineering of the learning experience (Cobb, Confrey, diSessa, Lehrer and Schauble 2003). The use of this tag is deliberate because proponents of design experiments see their origins in applied science, relying on a precise method that involves tinkering with the design of the intervention and learning from mistakes so the final product is finished to the highest standard. Just as with product design, the practitioners and researchers make minute adjustments to the specification, which they track in detail and perhaps adjust further over time. As Collins, Joseph and Bielaczyc write, 'the design is constantly revised based on experience, until all the bugs are worked out' (Collins, Joseph and Bielaczyc 2004: 8).

Design experiments explore and test hypotheses as in classic experimental research. But instead of the once-and-for-all hypothesis test (in the form of a statistical verification common in randomized controlled trials, which may confirm or reject the hypothesis) there is a quick turnover of research questions linked to the main hypothesis, followed by rapid redesigns of the intervention – what Cobb *et al.* call 'conjecture driven tests' (Cobb *et al.* 2003: 10). The idea is not to test general theories but to understand the practical limits and possibilities of what the innovation is trying to do. Design writers (Collins 1992; Collins *et al.* 2004) start with Simon's distinction in his book, *The Sciences of the Artificial*, between the type of theory building in the sciences of physics and biology, and that of the design sciences, or what he calls artificial sciences, such as engineering and computer science, which are more recent and where theory links to the tasks at hand. As Simon writes, 'We speak of engineering as concerned with "synthesis" whereas science is concerned with "analysis" ... The engineer, and more generally the designer, is concerned with how things *ought* to be – how they ought to be in order to *attain goals*' (Simon 1996: 4). Simon believes design scientists grapple with the complexity of the real world in a different way from their pure science colleagues. The theory in design experiments is intermediate, standing somewhere in between the grand statements of educational theory and accounts of practical relationships on the ground (diSessa 1991).

The researcher's role is like that of a participant. In fact, there is no reason why practitioners cannot be researchers; many design experiments are practitioner-run projects and, where there are researchers, there is a very close collaboration. Sometimes design experiments are known as design partnerships (http://www.soe.berkeley.edu/sandhtdocs/guide.html). In general, the person doing the design experiment participates in the innovation and in its evaluation. As Brown writes, 'As a design scientist in my field, I attempt to engineer innovative educational environments and simultaneously conduct experimental studies of those innovations' (Brown 1992: 141). Of course, researchers, like all participants, need to be alert to the potential conflict of interest between researchers and practitioners and the dangers of researchers going native and losing their claim to a scientific version of objectivity.

So far design experiments have mainly taken place in schools and their findings appear in specialist learning science journals. What scope is there for a more general application? Our starting point is that there is a case for transplanting the design experiment method to other contexts on the grounds that if it works in education, then it should work elsewhere. Indeed, we have carried out a design experiment on drugs policy (Askew, John and Liu 2010). Design experimenters who operate outside the classroom experience cannot have the same level of involvement in, and direction over, their environment as teachers and education researchers. It is more difficult to imagine researchers taking on the role of a social worker or police officer than a teacher. However, if the same amount of involvement is not possible in non-education environments, it is still possible to have close collaboration and involvement with the delivery of the project. Design experiments favour small-scale innovation, in a relatively controlled environment, where the dialogue can take place with a small range of policy-makers and workers, all of whom have signed up to the new way of doing business and to intense researcher-practitioner interactions. It is suited to policy being introduced in neighbourhoods or small areas without the fanfare and public scrutiny which would be given to a pilot area, where it is assumed there is a wider programme ready to be rolled out.

But many of these limitations of the design experiment method are, in fact, its advantages. Only policy-makers and practitioners who are committed both to a long-term evaluation and to creating innovation can work on design experiments, avoiding the problem of overload and expectations that are too high. By being more specialized, and targeted to the innovators, the design experiment encourages a high degree of focus and commitment in those who participate. It also biases the role of the policy-maker towards trying out more imaginative ways of intervening. The payoff is that the causal mechanisms can be understood much more clearly in relationship to the instruments the policy-makers have to hand. Other organizations and delivery bodies wishing to implement the policy innovation will not need to start from scratch.

## Conclusion

Experiments offer a powerful and robust way to evaluate interventions by public agencies and other people or bodies seeking to improve public welfare. The claim applies to both the randomized controlled trial and the design experiment. In either case, they provide warrantable knowledge for the academic, researcher and policy-maker. They offer a higher standard of knowledge through the systematic collection of evidence and the generation of the genuine counterfactual from which to compare the effect of an intervention. The randomized controlled trial allows the policy-maker and researcher to make an inference whether an intervention has worked or not, and by how much. This is the power of randomization: the only difference between the group that gets the intervention and the groups that does not is the intervention itself. Other methods do not come close in evaluating the policies of government because they permit factors other than the intervention to influence the outcomes a researcher or policy-maker observes, and it is almost impossible to control for these factors. Experiments are not a nirvana for reforming policy-makers and social scientists, and we have discussed their limitations earlier in this chapter. Some of the problems of randomized controlled trials can be overcome by effective piloting. Hence our advocacy of the design experiment as a qualitative complement to randomized controlled trials. Other limitations can be anticipated and corrected for in the design of the research, whereas the problems of other research methods cannot be successfully addressed. Doubt will always remain that something has not been allowed for, even in the most complex of statistical models.

What we have not communicated so far is that experiments can be great fun, being near to the real world with its challenges and thrills. Experimenters face the day-to-day up and downs far more than other researchers (and we should stress that getting experiments implemented is messy and unpredictable, as many of the following chapters show). Delivering an experiment requires considerable ingenuity and resourcefulness as well as sheer determination. There is the thrill of pulling off the research in the form of an effectively implemented intervention and control. Then there is the excitement of getting the results back. The clean nature of randomized controlled trials means that they do not rely on complex statistical procedures, such as multiple regression models, but on a simple comparison of outcomes that cannot be manipulated (though, of course, regression plays an important role in analysing experiments). The excitement of getting a positive result cannot be understated, but the disappointment of a null or negative result also has the compensation that it is a secure addition to knowledge. The design experiment has this real-world excitement, too, as there is close contact with policy-makers while they design and refine their interventions. Armed with these two methods, we are in a position to say whether think or nudge is the best route to civic behaviour and collective actions, and which aspects of these two ideas work best and by how much.

# 3

# Recycling

## Why study this topic?

The widespread provision of doorstep recycling collections and a growing public awareness of the challenges of dealing with climate change have, over the past decade, led to extensive change in behaviour. Many households now routinely sort their waste into a variety of containers provided by their local authority, ready for kerbside collection. But while most households have changed their behaviour, a significant minority do not participate, choosing to dispose of their recyclable waste in the household waste bin. Whilst kerbside collections of green waste, paper, cardboard, bottles and cans are now widely established in many parts of the developed world, public authorities have only recently started to introduce food waste collection schemes and are looking for ways to promote participation in this new service. Perhaps a gentle nudge can persuade households to sort their waste?

In this chapter we start by looking briefly at the current state of the evidence on what can nudge households to recycle. We then describe two randomized controlled trials, which test the impact of two different nudges on recycling behaviour. Both these experiments adopted a similar design: within a selected neighbourhood, half of the streets in the area were randomly assigned to receive an intervention to encourage recycling and the remaining streets were placed in a control group and received no special attention. Recycling participation rates for all households were measured before and after the intervention to see if the intervention had been effective. The first experiment tested the impact of door-to-door canvassing on recycling and the second tested the impact of 'smiley face' and 'frown face' feedback postcards on participation in a food waste collection scheme. In this chapter, we reflect on the findings from these two experiments and finish with a review of the lessons they offer for nudge strategies.

## What do we know about how to encourage recycling?

Research, using mainly observational data, shows that the design of a recycling service has an impact on participation, in particular the inclusion of a wide range of materials encourages participation (Harder, Woodard and Bench 2006; Woodward, Bench and Harder 2005). Offering appropriate containers also promotes recycling (Woodward *et al.* 2005). A box is probably easier for terraced houses which have storage and access issues, but wheeled bins will be more convenient for houses with driveways. Frequency of collection and day of collection have an impact, helping to encourage a routine or habit of recycling behaviour. Some recycling organizations alternate collections of recyclable and residual waste, with each being collected fortnightly on the same day in alternate weeks. This can work successfully (Wilson and Williams 2007) and challenges the public's perception that recycling is an add-on rather than a core feature of the waste system, but it can be controversial to cease weekly residual collections (Woodward *et al.* 2005). Vehicles collecting recycling waste should be visibly different from residual waste collection vehicles, so the public can trust that their recyclables will not end up in landfill sites (Woodward *et al.* 2005).

Promotional and educational campaigns can raise participation rates by ensuring that people understand the scheme and motivating people to get involved. High visibility events and road shows can be successful in building awareness (Read 1999). Incentives can work in areas with low recycling participation rates (Harder *et al.* 2006), but they may crowd out intrinsic motivation (Bryce, Day and Olney 1997); a survey of householders found that financial incentives are likely to be less effective in encouraging recycling than service improvements and active promotion (Shaw and Maynard 2008). Feedback cards left by collection crews to highlight boxes that contain contaminated material can be effective in reducing the amount of contamination and it is a cheap approach to adopt (Timlett and Williams 2008).

A study of five newspaper recycling schemes found that households are more likely to set out a recycling box if others in their street recycle regularly, but there is a danger that living on a street with high participation rates may encourage non- or infrequent recyclers to regularly recycle small amounts of material, rather than increasing the absolute amount of material recycled (Tucker 1999). One study found that households in shorter contiguous blocks (less than 15 houses) were influenced by the recycling actions of their nearest next-door neighbours, particularly in cul-de-sacs, but the influence of neighbours diminished as the length of the blocks increased (Shaw 2008). Harder *et al.* found that households on small roads tend to have a higher recycling participation rate (Harder *et al.*2006). Suggested factors include increased attachment to the neighbourhood, community spirit and peer pressure.

## Two randomized controlled trials to look at nudges and recycling

We tested two different types of nudge that might promote recycling behaviour: door-to-door canvassing and the provision of feedback. Previous studies of door-to-door canvassing suggest that is more effective in encouraging recycling than simply providing literature (Bryce *et al.* 1997; Reams and Ray 1993), but it is less effective in raising participation in areas where recycling is already high (over 60 per cent of households) (Timlett and Williams 2008). Doorstep canvassing has been found to increase voter turnout in elections by about 7 per cent in the UK (John and Brannan 2008; also see Chapter 5 of the current volume), replicating the treatment effects in US studies (Green and Gerber 2008).

The rationale behind the feedback approach is that most people underestimate the extent of pro-social behaviour among their peers and then use those low estimates as a standard against which to judge themselves (Schultz, Nolan, Cialdini, Goldstein and Griskevicius 2007). This assumes that people identify with groups and tend to emulate the behaviour of those they identify with (Tajfel and Turner 1986). Providing feedback is expected to lead to a general rise in pro-social behaviour by letting people know that the prevalence amongst their peers is higher than they thought. However, previous studies have shown mixed results. The provision of feedback on borough-wide recycling participation rates had no effect in changing householder behaviour in a London borough (Lyas, Shaw and Van Vugt 2004), but giving more specific feedback on the recycling activity of the individual household or the surrounding streets was successful in promoting recycling in the United States (Schultz 1998). The provision of written feedback on the election turnout of near neighbours had a substantial impact on encouraging voters to go to the polls, but the high effect of 8.1 per cent is linked to a shaming element to the intervention: households were told that their voting behaviour was being monitored and would be made public to their neighbours after the election (Gerber, Green and Larimer 2008). Feedback may have an unintended effect of discouraging those who already recycle, by alerting them that some of their neighbours are not participating. One solution to this is to include a smiley face or a frown face in the feedback, to let households know what is commonly approved or disapproved of within society (Reno, Cialdini and Kallgren 1993). Such an approach was tested in a field experiment on household energy use: adding a smiley face (☺) or a frown face (☹) encouraged both above-average consumers to reduce their energy use and below-average consumers to continue their low consumption rates (Schultz *et al.* 2007: 430).

## The impact of canvassing on household recycling

The randomized controlled trial set out to test whether door-to-door canvassing is effective in bringing about behaviour change on recycling (see Cotterill, John, Liu and Nomura 2009). The research was conducted in two adjoining neighbourhoods, Old Trafford and Gorse Hill, which are within the area of Trafford Metropolitan Borough Council, close to inner-city Manchester. The housing is a mixture of terraced and semi-detached houses. The area is relatively deprived and ethnically diverse compared to other areas nationally. A kerbside recycling service is provided by EMERGE, a social enterprise, which is commissioned by Trafford Metropolitan Borough Council to provide a weekly recycling service to all households. All the streets in Old Trafford and Gorse Hill that receive a recycling service from EMERGE were included in the research study. There are a total of 194 streets, with 6,580 households. Streets vary in size from 2 households to 190, with an average of 33.9 households per street. Flats and commercial properties were not included because they were not eligible for the recycling service.

The list of streets was randomly divided into two groups of equal size, one to be canvassed and the other to act as a control. The data was stratified by district (Old Trafford or Gorse Hill) and street length, prior to randomization. The treatment group contained 3,468 households in 97 streets and the control group contained 3,112 households in 97 streets. Random assignment was done at the street level rather than at the individual household level: we anticipated that canvassing one household might have an effect on the behaviour of its neighbours in the control group, which would contaminate the experiment. A street-based design reduced the possibility of such contamination.

One of four canvassers visited all households in the streets in the intervention group. The canvassing focused on three factors that are expected to influence recycling behaviour: awareness, attitudes and structural barriers (Shaw, Lyas, Maynard and Van Vugt 2007). Canvassers made sure householders were aware of the day and time of collection and the materials that can be recycled; they promoted positive attitudes to recycling; they addressed barriers to recycling by providing any plastic bags required and ordering new boxes if they were lost or missing. They dealt with any problems or queries about the service or passed any difficult queries on to an EMERGE manager. The canvassers were encouraged to be enthusiastic and conversational on the doorstep. They were provided with scripts to use as prompts but were encouraged to adapt them to their own conversational style. Canvassers were asked to take a different approach dependent on whether the householders were currently recyclers or non-recyclers. Canvassers thanked existing recyclers for using the recycling box, reminded them of the variety of recyclable materials and asked any enthusiastic householders if they would like to become recycling champions. Canvassers took a slightly different approach with non-recyclers, encouraging them to recycle, promoting the day and date of collection and providing information on the materials collected, before asking if they could be counted on to recycle regularly. An information leaflet was delivered to every household canvassed including those where no one was at home. The leaflet described what materials could be recycled, outlined the service provided, gave details of the time and day of collection and provided contact details for more information.

The canvassing took place over a period of six weeks in May and June 2008 between 3 p.m. and 7 p.m. Monday to Friday and 11 a.m. to 3 p.m. on Saturday. These times were chosen to maximize the number of contacts, based on previous best practice (Waste and Resources Action Programme 2006a). Our monitoring confirms that these times are suitable for a campaign of this type. Each street was canvassed twice. The second visits were arranged at a different time of day from the first visit to maximize contact. During the first canvass 40 per cent of households were spoken to. By the end of the second canvass, 61 per cent of households had been contacted: 2,129 of the 3,468 households in the intervention group. The contact rate compares favourably with other canvassing projects.

We measured recycling behaviour by observing which households put out a recycling container for collection. The monitoring was done on the same day as the waste collection. The monitor sat in the recycling vehicle while the crew were working and noted all the houses on the street that had placed recycling material outside the house boundary. The monitoring was repeated over three consecutive weeks: some households may not recycle weekly because of holidays or having low levels of recyclable waste. Any household that recycled at least once in the three-week period was counted as a recycler. This followed the most recent guidance from the Waste and Resources Action Programme, supported by the environment department, Defra (Waste and Resources Action Programme 2006b).

Participation in the recycling scheme was measured for all households in the intervention and control groups at three time points: in March–April 2008 prior to the canvassing, in July 2008 after its completion and in October 2008 to test whether households had got into the habit of recycling. Monitoring was not done on bank holidays (because services were disrupted) or during school holidays (when some households might be away). The task of monitoring participation, carried out three times, was done by a different person. None of these people were involved in any other aspect of the project and they were unaware which streets were in the treatment and control groups. The members of the recycling collection crew were aware of the research project, but did not know which streets were in the treatment and control groups.

Figure 3.1 compares the recycling participation rates of the control and canvass groups over time. At baseline, in March 2008, before the canvassing took place, the streets in the canvass group had an average participation rate of 48 per cent compared to 54 per cent of the control group. By July, immediately after the canvassing, the recycling participation rate of the canvassed streets rose to 52 per cent, a rise of 4 per cent, and participation in the control group dropped to 53 per cent, a fall of 1 per cent. The randomization of the two groups means that the streets in the canvass group are the same as those in the control group in every respect except for having been canvassed, so we should assume that – without the canvassing – the recycling rates of the canvass group would have fallen by 1 per cent, the same as the control group. Overall the short-term effect of the canvassing campaign was to raise recycling by 5 per cent (four plus 1 per cent).

**Figure 3.1**  Recycling participation rate by group.

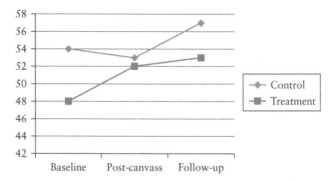

Between the baseline monitoring in March 2008 and the follow up monitoring in October, the average participation rate of the canvassed streets rose from 48 per cent to 53 per cent, a rise of 5 percentage points and the control group rose from 54 per cent to 57 per cent, a rise of 3 percentage points. So, overall the longer-term effect of the canvassing campaign was to raise recycling by 2 percentage points (5 minus 3 per cent).

Similar canvassing campaigns conducted by the Waste and Resources Action Programme have led to immediate rises in participation of 9.6 per cent in Braintree District Council (estimate based on provisional results), 6.5 per cent in Essex County Council and 7 per cent in Luton Borough Council. However, none of these studies included a control group, so there is no way of knowing whether these rises were the result of the canvassing or some other factors and none included a follow-up measure to test the impact over time (Waste and Resources Action Programme 2006a). The only academic study of a canvassing campaign found an overall fall of 4 per cent, but again there was no control group (Timlett and Williams 2008).

We can sum up: a door-to-door canvassing campaign can successfully raise participation in a kerbside recycling scheme by 5 per cent. The effect is still there three months later, but is reduced to 2 per cent, showing a decline over time. This might suggest that canvassing and other promotional campaigns need to be repeated regularly to reinforce the recycling message. The canvassing had less impact on streets where recycling rates were already very high. The canvassing campaign was more successful in the most deprived neighbourhoods and in neighbourhoods with a large ethnic minority population. Canvassing campaigns are likely to be most successful if targeted in streets with low baseline recycling rates, in relatively deprived areas and in neighbourhoods with a high proportion of ethnic minorities.

## The impact of feedback on food waste recycling

The randomized controlled trial set out to test whether feedback cards are effective in bringing about behaviour change on food waste recycling (see Nomura, Cotterill and John 2010). The research was undertaken in Oldham, a former mill town in Greater Manchester. Oldham Council provides waste collection services to all households in the borough, with separate collections of garden waste, mixed recyclables, residual waste and a weekly collection of food waste. Among the nine councils in Greater Manchester, Oldham was the first to collect food waste, and the implementation of the scheme is being watched with interest by neighbouring authorities. The research was undertaken in the autumn of 2009. Oldham Council offers a food waste collection service to 89,000 households. The sample consisted of all the households covered by six separate collection rounds, located in different parts of the town: 318 streets with 9,082 households. Streets vary in size from 1 household to 229, with an average of 62 households per street. Flats and commercial properties are not included because they are not eligible for the recycling service.

The list of streets was randomly divided into two groups of equal size, one to receive feedback and the other to act as a control. The data was stratified by collection round (six rounds), recycling performance at baseline (above or below the average) and street size prior to randomization. The treatment group contained 5,009 households in 159 streets and the control group contained 4,073 households in 159 streets.

Postcards where delivered to each household in the treatment group providing feedback on how their street performed compared to the average for their neighbourhood. Giving feedback is a classic nudge. The leaflet stated: 'Did you know: X per cent of homes on A Street recycle their food waste. The average for the area is Y per cent'. It included either a smiley face (☺) or a frown face (☹), depending on whether the street was better or worse than the neighbourhood average, and it concluded with the message: 'With your help your street could become the best recycling street in Oldham.' On the reverse were details of how to participate in the food waste scheme. The contents of the card were tailored to each street, and were produced using the data gathered by monitoring participation. The feedback postcards were delivered twice: once during the week after the first round of participation monitoring and again the week after the second round of monitoring. The feedback cards were delivered by EMERGE recycling. Households in the treatment group could receive the following possible combinations of feedback:

Smiley card at time one – smiley card at time two (smiley-smiley)
Smiley card at time one – frown card at time two (smiley-frown)
Frown card at time one – frown card at time two (frown-frown)
Frown card at time one – smiley card at time two (frown-smiley)

The participation of all households in both the feedback and the control groups was monitored. The method was similar to the previous experiment: a monitor travelled ahead of the collection crew and noted all the houses that had placed a food-waste bin outside the house boundary. The monitoring was repeated over three consecutive weeks and a household was counted as participating if they put out a container at least one week in three. The monitoring was undertaken by EMERGE recycling. Participation in the scheme was measured for all households at three time points: in August 2009 prior to the feedback campaign, in September 2009 after the delivery of the first feedback postcard and in October 2009 after receiving the second postcard.

**Figure 3.2** Proportion of households recycling food waste

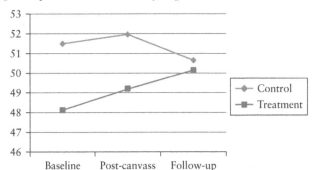

Figure 3.2 compares the recycling participation rate of the control and feedback groups. At baseline, before the feedback cards were sent, the streets in the treatment group had a mean participation rate of 48.1 per cent, compared to 51.5 per cent in the control group. After two feedback cards were sent, recycling participation of the treatment streets rose to 50.1 per cent, a rise of 2 per cent, and participation in the control group dropped to 50.6 per cent, a fall of 1 per cent. The randomization of the two groups meant that the streets in the feedback group were the same as those in the control group in every respect except for having been sent feedback, so we should assume that – without the feedback – the recycling rates of the feedback group would have fallen by 1 per cent, the same as the control group. So, overall the short-term effect of the feedback was to raise recycling by 3 per cent (2 per cent plus 1 per cent). In summary, providing feedback cards to households on their street's performance raised participation in the food waste scheme by 3 percentage points, compared to a control group. Both smiley and frown feedback were effective: positive feedback encouraged those in high-performing streets to carry on making the effort, while negative feedback persuaded those in low-performing streets to join in with the food waste collection scheme.

The only situation in which feedback was found not to be effective was with households who were already participating in the scheme. For some of the households who were already putting out their food waste, the feedback acted to discourage them from carrying on. We speculate that this is because people who were already making the effort to sort their food waste were discouraged by cards that said their street does not follow their personal behaviour.

Smaller streets were more likely to recycle and we found that feedback was more effective on smaller streets than longer streets. However, this effect was quite small. Feedback was most effective when given more than once, to reiterate the message, and when the feedback was consistent: households who received two smiley cards or two frown cards were more likely to respond than those who received mixed messages.

## What are the lessons for a nudge strategy?

The two recycling experiments have the following implications for a nudge strategy. The first implication is the importance of group loyalty and identification. The findings from the food waste experiment indicate that the length of the street has an impact on recycling behaviour. People on small streets are more likely to recycle, perhaps because their behaviour is more observable to others whom they know. Secondly, the feedback cards had a greater impact on shorter streets, suggesting that there is greater group identification on smaller streets, with households being more influenced by messages about the behaviour of others when the reference group is small. However, a limitation of the nudge is that, although statistically significant, both these effects are fairly small. Similar street effects were not found in the recycling experiment. Overall, it seems likely from this, and other research, that household recycling behaviour is influenced by the actions of close neighbours, but the street may not be the best reference group, because streets are so variable in their size and make-up: the focus should perhaps be on the immediate circle of neighbouring properties.

The food waste experiment confirms that behaviour can be shaped by the use of relevant social or community influences. Households in both high-performing and low-performing streets were persuaded to improve or maintain their behaviour when given information on the recycling performance of their street compared to a wider neighbourhood. However, a limitation of this nudge is that feedback cards were not effective if households were already recycling their food waste at baseline: we assume that people are discouraged if they learn that they are performing better than the norm for their street. Future feedback campaigns are likely to be most effective if targeted at those whose behaviour needs to change, rather than as a way of sustaining those who are already engaged in pro-social behaviour.

The second implication of recycling research for a nudge strategy is for the discussion on choice architecture. Previous research has found that the design of the waste collection scheme is an important element in encouraging people to take part: a scheme that is easy to use, efficient and can be trusted is more likely to be well used by residents. Citizens often regard their own behaviour change as part of a contract with expectations on both sides: if citizens are to consider changing their behaviour, they will have high expectations about the behaviour of public agencies. While this was not directly tested in this research, it was observed during the experiment that the canvassing campaign coincided with a period when the recycling collection crew was short-staffed and there was a reliance on casual staff. A minority of householders complained of missed collections, rude staff, dirty boxes and pedantry over contamination. These households had given up on recycling altogether and had to be persuaded to restart. Canvassers felt they had to win people round who were fed up with the service, as one canvasser commented: if 'collections weren't right or something went wrong or they got disenchanted because they don't get their bin back or they are confused about how things should be sorted ... we have tried to persuade them to give it another go'.

The canvassers were negotiating a contract with the householder: persuading people to recycle in expectation that the service would be better than before. By the time of the final monitoring in October 2008, a permanent and settled collection crew was in place, and the level of participation rallied to a higher level than at baseline.

These studies indicate the usefulness of adopting nudge strategies to promote recycling, but they also suggest limitations to nudge, which should be taken into account when designing campaigns. When using approaches based on social influences, it is important to consider what might be the most appropriate reference group, within which group loyalties may develop: the reference group may vary between individuals and may not conform to established geographic boundaries. Nudge strategies may need to be targeted, with different approaches being made to those who already participate in pro-social behaviour and those who have not yet engaged. Nudges are low-level interventions that will not automatically lead to a long-term change of habit, so they can work best if repeated regularly to reinforce the message.

*Further reading*
The best study is Schultz, P.W. (1998), 'Changing Behaviour with Normative Feedback Interventions: Field Experiment on Kerbside Recycling', *Basic and Applied Psychology*, 21: 25–36. For advice on how to organize a door-

to-door canvassing campaign: Waste and Resources Action Programme (2006a), *Step by Step Guide to Door–to-door Canvassing,* http://www. wrap.org.uk. For guidance on how to monitor household participation in recycling: Waste and Resources Action Programme (2006b) *Improving the Performance of Waste Diversion Schemes: A Good Practice Guide to Monitoring and Evaluation,* http://www.wrap.org.uk.

# 4

# Volunteering

## Why try to increase volunteering?

The idea of co-production is that public services and citizens contribute jointly to deliver positive social outcomes and sympathetic environments in which people can have creative, productive and fulfilling lives (see, for example, Boyle and Harris 2009). Underlying recent interest in co-production across the political spectrum is a belief that 60 years of state provision of welfare, however well-intentioned, has eaten away at citizens' capacity and desire for mutuality and for self-help. These are not new ideas. William Beveridge, seen by many as the founder of the British welfare state, argued in 1948 for the importance of the 'mutual aid motive in action' and the 'philanthropic motive in action' (Beveridge 1948). He was 'keen to recognize that the state could and should have a vital and proactive role in developing policy frameworks to nurture both solidaristic and sympathetic human motivations and their capacities for expression' (Kendall 2009: 3). In Beveridge's view, the state's role was to exercise self-restraint, and voluntarism would balance the power and dominance of the state.

There have been well-documented shifts in the types of civic activity in which people engage; preferences for new individualized and consumer-based expressions of solidarity and philanthropy have arguably overtaken traditional forms such as volunteering. So, new activities such as boycotting or 'buycotting' consumer goods on political or ethical grounds, or wearing badges and wristbands for causes, are on the rise internationally (Micheletti 2010). However, there remains a firm interest in getting citizens to participate in co-production through active volunteering. For many policy outcomes, action by the state cannot substitute for civic acts. For example, local efforts by public sector bodies to clear up unsightly bulky refuse (like mattresses and fridges) are not a substitute for citizens choosing not to dispose of unwanted items by dumping, and preferably by citizens also assisting with the process through clean-up days and similar exercises. Volunteering is also not easily replaced by other civic acts, such as ethical buying, which may be driven by similar sympathetic human motivations, and towards similar solidaristic ends, but which do not offer the potential for co-produced outcomes.

In this chapter we review the evidence on promoting volunteering. The chapter contains summaries of the various options that have been tried and a discussion of what a nudge strategy could offer. It examines a particular case and reports from a design experiment in an English local authority which attempted to facilitate volunteering by asking citizens who complain to a local authority telephone call centre to do other civic-minded acts. What do these findings imply for the challenge of promoting volunteering? By changing the choice architecture can you turn complainers to volunteers?

## What do we already know? How much volunteering already exists?

There have been numerous policy interventions by public institutions, in the UK and internationally, to encourage volunteering. In the ten years from 1997/1998 to 2007/2008, UK central government investment in adult volunteering increased five-fold (Das-Gupta 2008). Youth volunteering policy has seen marketing of the V brand, and the creation of a national youth citizenship scheme. Beyond the UK, 2011 was the United Nations' and the European Union's International Year of Volunteering.

Is Britain different from elsewhere? In the United States, data from the US Bureau of Labor Statistics show that 26.8 per cent of the population volunteered through, or for, an organization at least once between September 2008 and September 2009 (Corporation for National and Community Service 2010). These figures were down slightly from 27.4 per cent in 2002 and highs of 28.8 per cent between 2003 and 2005, but an increase from 26.2 per cent in 2007 and 26.4 per cent in 2008 (Corporation for National and Community Service 2006). Despite these dips, the overall rate of volunteering in the United States is similar to that in the United Kingdom, where 28 per cent of people were engaged in regular formal volunteering in 2009, with no change between 2001 and 2009 (Department for Communities and Local Government 2009). Occasional formal volunteering showed an increase from 39 per cent in 2001 to 43 per cent in 2009. There were decreases in occasional informal volunteering (from 67 per cent in 2001 to 57 per cent in 2009) and regular informal volunteering (from 37 per cent in 2003 to 33 per cent in 2009) (Department for Communities and Local Government 2009). It is important to be cautious about these results as they are based on survey reports and may not be accurate measures of actual behaviour.

Reliable and consistent trend data in nearly all countries are not longitudinal and therefore do not show how many drop out and how many join in. Given a wide range in the lengths of time spent volunteering, these figures may represent many more individuals contributing over the period than is apparent. Volunteering levels of between 26 and 57 per cent indicate an arguably healthy base of citizen activity, but with potential to drive up levels particularly on regular formal volunteering.

## The literature – how can volunteering be increased?

It is not immediately clear what else, if anything, could be done to raise volunteering rates. However, there are some clues in the literature. Verba, Schlozman and Brady's study of facilitators of civic voluntarism outlines a civic voluntarism model, which sets out three drivers to stimulate volunteering: capacity; motivation and mobilization (being asked) (Verba, Schlozman and Brady 1995). In this model, mobilizing is effective where: 'people are resource-rich, have plenty of free time and have a strong sense of efficacy' or interest already (Pattie and Seyd 2003: 446). Mobilization is predicated on sufficient capacity and motivation.

How could these ideas be translated into possible nudges to increase volunteering? The presumptions in the civic voluntarism model offered some interesting areas to test using the idea of nudge. Was there an untapped pool of unasked, skilled and keen people who could be more effectively mobilized than through previous interventions? Could the predicates be reversed or bypassed? Was it necessary to build up or rely on pre-existing capacity and motivation, or could mobilization through a nudge develop capacity and motivation? Mobilizing is a classic nudge strategy, as it presumes citizens might already be able and willing but not activated, or could become more able and willing if activated.

Someone or something needs to be the mobilizer and do the asking. In the original civic voluntarism model, mobilization is done through 'networks of recruitment' (Verba et al. 1995: 3) and interpersonal relationships, primarily informal recruitment through friends, acquaintances and colleagues, but also political parties. The workplace, churches and voluntary associations act as the 'loc[i] of recruitment' (Verba et al. 1995: 144). Verba et al. discuss the 'non-political secondary institutions of adult life – the workplace, voluntary associations, or church' (Verba et al. 1995: 369). These institutions are crucial, mostly insofar as the settings in which mobilization happens are where colleagues gather and have conversations and where 'psychological engagement' (motivation) is cultivated through debate and other cues and hooks. These settings are also where transferable skills (capacity) are acquired. Formal requests by institutions play only a small role. Later work by Lowndes, Pratchett and Stoker extends the model and sets out an enhanced formal role for institutions as mobilizers in their own right, and as mobilizers of a wider group of citizens than the institutions' members or employees (Lowndes,

Pratchett and Stoker 2006). They propose the CLEAR framework (see Table 4.1): Can do – that is, have the resources and knowledge to participate; Like to – that is, have a sense of attachment that reinforces participation; Enabled to – that is, are provided with the opportunity for participation; Asked to – that is, are mobilized by official bodies or voluntary groups; and Responded to – that is, see evidence that their views have been considered.

**Table 4.1** The CLEAR model

| |
|---|
| **Can do** – have the resources and knowledge to participate |
| **Like to** – have a sense of attachment that reinforces participation |
| **Enabled to** – are provided with the opportunity for participation |
| **Asked to** – are mobilized through public or voluntary groups |
| **Responded to** – see evidence that their views have been considered |

Source: Adapted from Lowndes, Pratchett and Stoker 2006

Existing practice by local government institutions as official bodies suggests a limited and not fully effective mobilizing role. Local government advertises local events and activities, and most contribute funding to Volunteer Bureaux. Data produced for 2007/ 2008 shows that 3 per cent of adults found out about volunteering opportunities from Volunteer Bureaux, under 10 per cent through advertising and over half by word of mouth (Agur and Low 2009: 166). At the same time, each local government body conducts thousands of direct transactions with citizens and service users, but does not use these contact points as mobilizing opportunities. Moreover, a high proportion of the transactions are initiated by the citizen, many because something has gone wrong with public services. The citizen or service user contacts a local authority with a one-way request for the public body to solve a problem, for example a person rings a customer contact centre direct to request that street cleaners come to their neighbourhood and remove litter from streets.

A civic request is not made of residents during these routine service interactions. There may well be a reciprocal civic request being made of the same citizens by the same institution, for example, to join in a neighbourhood clean-up day. But the institution's request is often made by a different department, at a different time, through an indirect route (for example, posters at a local school), and usually generates extremely low returns. When a citizen calls a local authority contact centre, the presumption by the authority appears to be that their behaviour is not civic. Yet the person being treated as a customer may be acting as a good citizen, hoping their phone call will lead to neighbourhood improvements, cleaner streets or better neighbourhood relations. Even if a call is not orientated towards improving public goods, or influencing the institution more generally, there is still a possibility that the caller would be willing to consider making this sort of contribution, if they were asked. Therefore, the potential for co-production is often lost.

## What is the intervention? The nudge experiment

When citizens do get mobilized through being upset about the streets not being cleaned or bins not been emptied, the public authority can use such a situation to nudge citizens into more civic-minded behaviour. The nudge experiment was undertaken by the University of Manchester working in partnership with a local authority. The idea was to see if voluntary activity could be mobilized more effectively. The partners agreed to change the choice architecture: the default settings of the institution – the local council in this case – were changed from one that assumed that citizens have a largely passive rule to one where they have a fuller relationship with public authorities and their communities, and would want to become volunteers. The original default setting was that routine service transactions were with service users as passive complainers and consumers. This was altered to a new default setting that any interaction was with potentially active citizens. This also required changes in the organization's cultural default settings. Seeing the callers as complaining customers suggested that the council anticipated customer hostility to being asked to volunteer. Regarding people as both consumers and potential co-producers required the council to presume people would be comfortable with being asked.

To test this out, the experiment was focused on promoting voluntary activity in two neighbourhoods in a Blackburn. Callers reporting a problem or making a query to a local authority customer contact centre were asked if they wanted to get more involved in the neighbourhood. Typical reasons for calling were complaints about environmental services. After the query or complaint had been dealt with, citizens from those neighbourhoods who telephoned the contact centre were asked: 'We are currently promoting civic awareness in [your neighbourhood] and are looking for people to get involved in improving the area. We want to encourage people to take action on community issues in the area. Would you be interested in finding out more?'

Citizens who were identified as interested were split into two groups. Half of the potential volunteers were allocated randomly to an intervention group which was then encouraged – using a variety of approaches – to take further steps such as joining a local group, becoming volunteers or changing their environmental behaviour. The other half of the volunteers were allocated to a comparison group who were sent an information pack on opportunities for civic participation in the neighbourhood. The information pack contained information that was already publicly available and marketed to residents, and, as such, was similar to a placebo treatment.

There were two waves of the experiment. In the first, existing opportunities to participate were unchanged; what was new was the proactive approach by the contact centre, combined with a local neighbourhood officer, providing information and encouragement to the intervention group. In the second, the follow-up contact with the neighbourhood officer was supplemented by the creation of new volunteering opportunities for the intervention group. All participants were interviewed at the start of the project, and again eight weeks later, and were asked about civic activity and attitudes. These new volunteering activities were then offered to the comparison group after the data collection had been completed.

The first phase occurred in April–July 2008 in one neighbourhood. During this first phase, the intervention was tweaked in response to the research findings. Using the lessons from the first wave, the experiment was repeated in a second neighbourhood. The second phase took place between February and August 2009 in a different neighbourhood. A steering group for the project included the manager of the contact centre, the head of customer services and three members of the council's neighbourhood team, a housing association manager, a policy manager and the researchers. The steering group met regularly to reflect on the emerging findings from the research and decide whether the intervention should be tweaked to improve its effectiveness. The aim was to identify the most effective and appropriate way to design the intervention, both in the contact centre and in the neighbourhood.

The actual research took place in Blackburn in northwest England. The first neighbourhood was a residential area, relatively deprived in national terms, but fairly affluent compared to surrounding areas of the town. The housing was mostly owner-occupied or privately rented. The area had a high ethnic minority population, mostly of Pakistani and Bangladeshi family heritage. The area was chosen as a suitable for this experiment because it had an active and welcoming community association together with a range of other potential activities. The second neighbourhood was less affluent, within the lowest 5 per cent of neighbourhoods in England, and was among the most deprived in the borough. It was a predominantly white, former council estate, now managed by a housing association. Most of the properties were social housing, with pockets of owner-occupation. Over 40 per cent of households claimed state benefits. The experiment included all telephone callers from the neighbourhood to the council's contact centre complaining about cleansing, environment or neighbourhood services. During the second wave, calls about council tax and housing benefits were also included.

## The results

There were two critical successes that suggest the potential for a nudge strategy to change complainers into volunteers. The first was that citizens welcomed the change in the choice architecture. From the start of the research, there had been some concern from local authority staff that there would be an adverse reaction from citizens to this change of approach. In particular, the contact centre managers were worried that people phoning to report problems or make complaints might be irritated by being invited to be proactive on neighbourhood issues; those reporting a problem with a local service would be angry at being asked to take action themselves. Members of staff were not convinced that people would welcome a change in the nature of the relationship.

These concerns over the change in the default setting were not borne out by citizens' responses. The research tested the assumptions about citizens' preferences. The doubts of members of staff proved to be unfounded among those citizens who took part. People were happy to be mobilized by public institutions. Citizens were generally supportive, with 92 per cent across both intervention and comparison groups agreeing that the council should encourage callers to get more involved. One person spoke about the importance of the council working in partnership with members of the public:

> They [the council] are restricted in what they can do. They should work with the people to get to the bottom of it rather than tell people to ring somewhere else. We raise the same issue repeatedly and no records are kept. They probably live in the community and can benefit. We need to step back and see each others' perspectives.

The research also looked at people's motives for wanting to get involved, and found that they supported the change in default setting. People's motives did appear to be broadly concerned with public goods such as community safety or environmental conditions, and therefore could be classified as civic: most people wanted to make a difference in the area. Seven of the 30 participants in the first iteration were motivated by a principled feeling that everyone should do their bit, which is an explicitly stated belief in co-production: for example, 'I think I should be not just complaining, actually doing something' and 'If you're not making an effort you can't complain'. Where people were concerned, it was scepticism about how far the institution was making a genuine change: 'Worried it's just a token gesture'. Others were sceptical about to what extent the project could overcome barriers to participation, and argued that other citizens would not respond: 'They are flogging a dead horse' and 'it will fall on deaf ears'.

The second critical success was that the initial nudge did start to mobilize people towards volunteering. The request by the contact centre generated additional interest from citizens who had not previously been involved in volunteering, and was successful in attracting a cross-section of people in the neighbourhood. In neighbourhood one, 30 callers were recruited, including Asian women, younger people and a large proportion of people in work. Five people had not undertaken any civic activity in the past year and a further 11 had only done limited, one-off activity. In neighbourhood two the profile was different, reflecting differences in the local population. Of the 33 callers recruited, all were white, and compared to the callers in the first location, participants tended to be slightly older. Only a quarter were in work and a third were sick or disabled or caring for a sick or disabled relative. Seventeen had not taken part in any civic activity in the past year and a further nine had only done limited, one-off activity.

However, the initial surge in interest was not translated into activity. The comparison group performed as well as the intervention group in carrying out voluntary activity, and neither group showed massive increases. The nudge was in two iterations: changing the way the authority mobilized through the contact centre, with a light-touch follow-up using existing volunteering opportunities; then a second iteration which also created new volunteering opportunities. The fundamental initial shift in the default setting at the contact centre created a different citizen response. But the experiment failed to capitalize on the initial expression of interest in the follow-up intervention. There were several reasons for this. One obvious argument is that when put on the spot, people gave socially acceptable responses without being genuinely committed to considering civic action. Therefore, interest tails off. While this is always possible, there are more cogent arguments that may explain the drop-off in citizen interest.

The neighbourhood officers did not make contact with eight of the seventeen people in the intervention group, meaning that the intervention was flawed. More importantly, in the follow-up interviews people fed back that the voluntary opportunities offered in the first wave were not appropriate ones. For example, the types of voluntary contributions in which people expressed interest included making themselves available to present their views, or having a more in-depth dialogue with services, in order that services could better tailor, or adapt, their responses. This could include expanding the presence of police community support officers or improving parking or helping to improve the appearance of the area by reducing the amount of litter or rubbish dumping. It could include citizens helping to improve things as individuals, for example by improving their own front gardens, or by running practical community projects to help each other, such as neighbourhood watch schemes ('We should be vigilant and help each other') and projects to reduce the isolation of elderly and housebound people.

No one explicitly mentioned wanting to attend meetings or join existing community groups. Indeed, some participants had previously been put off volunteering through their experience or knowledge of these existing opportunities. However, in the first wave, the options offered to interested citizens were largely about attending public meetings or joining local community associations to help with their limited range of activities, in tightly prescribed roles. There were few options that fitted people's preferences. For example, no support was offered for garden tidying, and there were no creative ways for people to have dialogue with service providers other than the conventional routes of public meetings or individual complaints. There was some assistance offered to those wanting to set up mutual aid and self-help community projects, but it was to transfer the job of mobilizing on to the citizen, so people were given information packs for neighbourhood watch schemes, but were not given the names of other residents who had also expressed an interest. Residents said they were uncomfortable with the level of administration involved in setting up a scheme.

The second wave of the experiment was adapted to address this, using the things citizens had said they wanted to do in order to develop new options. For those wanting to use their views more constructively to improve services, the authority then started to set up the public sector equivalent of a mystery shopping exercise. It had previously used mystery shopping with paid staff, but wanted to extend this to citizens. People are offered training before using a script to make a series of requests of the authority, and the response is recorded using a set of criteria. Tests are made using different scenarios, from different types of citizen, with different staff and departments. Feedback is then given on how well the authority performed and on areas for improvement. However, the process of creating the scheme was a long and involved one, requiring agreement at a senior level on the timing of the mystery shopping exercise, its parameters, the script used and feedback mechanisms, as well as organizing a relatively expensive specialist training package for the volunteers which took place over an induction period.

For those wanting to offer help to neighbours, the authority facilitated a good neighbour scheme through which residents could offer social support to isolated older people by means of a good morning phone call. This involved many weeks of work by the council to identify vulnerable older people who may need help, advertise the service to them and set up training in befriending for the volunteers.

Therefore, although progress was made on creating new volunteering opportunities, the delays in doing this meant that momentum was lost, and citizens' initial fears that the institutional change would not be deep enough seemed to be confirmed. The nudge did not go far enough in changing the choice architecture. Feedback from citizens suggests that mobilization would have resulted in more activity had the changes been more extensive.

## Discussion – could we have improved the nudge?

Could the nudge have been improved? What would have made it a better nudge? Arguably, the experiment needed to go further by changing all aspects of the choice architecture, and doing this more quickly. The change in default setting did not extend quickly enough to volunteering options. The original intention was to offer a creative menu of voluntary options based on individuals' skills and interests. However, the institution reverted to a default setting previously hidden, which was co-production options that suited the institution and its skill set, rather than options tailored to the citizen. Participants in the first-wave intervention were offered an arguably uninspiring menu of involvement in existing neighbourhood groups and forums – easy for the authority to understand, based on a established repertoire of engagement skills, known entities, low supervision and transaction costs – though citizens would have preferred stronger voice mechanisms, less group-reliant activities requiring additional organization, higher monitoring and transaction costs, and innovative thinking. In the language of the CLEAR model, people were not 'enabled to'; the choices we tilted people towards were not attractive or tailored enough. By the second wave, the authority had started to develop new options, but this was too slow for many of the people we had mobilized.

Another issue was that the experiment focused on changing default settings, but neglected other elements of nudging, in particular the incentives, structuring complex choices, giving feedback and expecting error. If volunteering had been incentivized, for example through Timebanking (a scheme where volunteers earn time credits to spend later on, see http://www. timebanking.org) or childcare offers, this may have increased activity. There was a gap in helping practitioners and citizens structure complex choices. Both parties know they wanted volunteering to happen, but neither was clear how best this could be done. Both had identified problems they wanted to tackle, but were unsure how to go about this. We started to help people structure these choices, first by getting local authority staff to conduct a skills audit with citizens, and then holding a workshop discussion with staff to take account of these skills and interests in developing a more extensive menu of options for citizens. Nudge includes the idea of feedback, which was used in the experiment but too late to have any real feedback effects. The authority did give feedback to people in the experiment (or 'responded to them' in CLEAR terminology) about how many other citizens had participated, and thanked them in an effort to validate citizens' efforts in coming forward. We have seen and can understand some of the gaps in the experiment in terms of nudge ideas. But as well as offering a way of interpreting our results, nudge is a potential tool for strengthening the activity. The likelihood is that a stronger nudge may have been able to extend the results further.

*Further reading*
The CLEAR framework is explained in Lowndes, V., Pratchett, L. and Stoker, G. (2006), 'Diagnosing and Remedying the Failings of Official Participation Schemes: the CLEAR framework', *Social Policy and Society*, 5: 281–91. The citizen perspective on volunteering is captured in Lowndes, V., Pratchett, L. and Stoker, G. (2001), 'Trends in Public Participation: Part 2 – Citizens' Perspectives', *Public Administration*, 79: 445–55. A review of citizen-sponsored efforts at community action is Richardson, L. (2008), *DIY Community Action. Neighbourhood Problems and Community Self-help*, Bristol: Policy Press. Fung, A. (2006), *Empowered Participation: Reinventing urban Democracy*, Princeton, NJ: Princeton University Press provides a comparative perspective on empowerment.

# 5

# Voting

## Why is political participation important?

If the pessimists are to be believed, Britain and other democracies are experiencing a crisis of political participation when it is very hard to engage citizens in conventional forms of politics, such as voting in elections. Citizens appear to be turned off by political parties and politicians, and have disengaged from politics as a result. This is often seen as the result of a more privatized, work intensive and mobile society (Putnam 2000); it may also be the result of the declining performance of democracies, which have not fulfilled citizen expectations, and where politicians have not kept their promises (Putnam and Pharr 2000). This could be the fault of the politicians, in particular their inappropriate use of public funds, highlighted, for example, by the furore over the expense claims of UK Members of Parliament in 2009. Or it might be to do with the unrealistic expectations – inevitably dashed – which citizens have of politicians (Stoker 2006).

In the introduction, we alluded to the idea that there is no crisis of civic participation, pointing to the continuing interest citizens have in politics and the large variety of citizen activities that are either continuing at similar levels or extending into new areas (Dalton 2004; Pattie, Seyd and Whiteley 2005). But it remains the case that citizen participation in some forms of conventional political activities, such as voting and membership of political parties, has declined. However, is there a cause for concern if democracy still seems to function in much the same way, even with less people as members of political parties and less people voting in elections? It also might not be the most direct way of addressing problems of collective action, as voting in elections does not get directly to the social, economic and environmental problems a society like the UK faces. More people voting does not lead to more recycling. However, there may be many reasons for increasing political participation alongside the civic acts we describe in other chapters, particularly so that collective decisions can be made by a wider group than a self-selected minority of citizens. In addition, the actions the state takes to involve citizens might lack legitimacy if many of the same people who are expected to recycle more or care more for their neighbours are not represented in the larger collective decisions. Where citizens own the policies made in their name, government seems less technocratic and manipulative when asking citizens to do more (though it is slightly paradoxical that governments manipulate political participation in order to prevent citizens feeling manipulated by government!).

So what can public agencies to do to mobilize citizens? Here there are some different choices. In the think camp, the task is about using deliberative mechanisms to promote citizen interest and engagement with politics. From this perspective, the key to raising citizen interest is through creating open forums and arenas whereby citizens may debate issues and make decisions about public policy, preferably on equal terms with each other. By giving citizens a direct voice in decision-making, it is expected that citizen interest and engagement would increase. The nudge perspective says something different. It may be the case that citizens are well disposed to participate, thinking that voting in elections is a good thing, as are other forms of participation in politics, but, for a variety of reasons to do with busyness and forgetfulness, they fail to do them. What citizens need is a cue, an encouragement that gets them to participate and which they appreciate. In some ways, this is similar to the canvassing argument made in Chapter 3 that citizens can be encouraged to do something civic (such as recycle their waste) by someone knocking on their doors and seeking their views on the subject.

To make this argument, this chapter first reviews the experimental literature on citizen mobilization, then reports an experiment that we carried out to mobilize citizens. It concludes by reviewing the potential of nudges to raise political participation.

## What do we know about mobilizing to vote?

Voting usually draws on long-term factors that draw people into politics, such as the influence of parents and the family context. Of critical importance is socio-economic background, such as age, sex, ethnicity and income, all of which combine to give individuals more resources for getting involved and developing an interest in politics (Pattie *et al.* 2005). In attempting to mobilize people to vote, it is not possible – at least in the short term – to change the level of resources associated with socio-economic status, though it may be possible to tailor campaigns to take account of different socio-economic groups in society. More likely to change is the response of individuals to the strategic context in which they vote, such as the closeness of the race, which has a well-known effect on turnout. Voters go to the polls when they think the margins are close. However, it is not possible to manipulate this, except through a change to the electoral system, and that argument is beyond the scope of this book. It would be possible to manipulate the information voters get about the closeness of the electoral context, for example by deliberately informing them that a race is close. But this would raise ethical concerns and it is better to accept the electoral context as it is, and to appeal to voters' interests and their sense of duty in relation to voting.

Gerber, Green and colleagues tested for the effects of Get Out the Vote campaigns in a series of pioneering field experiments which show that a face-to-face contact from a non-partisan source, carried out by members of a field force calling at the homes of citizens and seeking to persuade them to vote, can increase voter turnout (see Green and Gerber 2008). Further experiments find that telephoning has an impact ranging from ineffective to positive, depending on the nature of the call. There are positive, if weaker, results for other forms of intervention, such as door postings and leafleting, none for email, and weakly positive or null impacts from rote telephoning (Green and Gerber 2008). Many of these results derive from single cases or from a limited number of research sites; however, the collating of these findings allows political scientists to be confident of the impacts. Although Get Out the Vote studies of this kind cannot adjudicate authoritatively on why the nudge works, the difference in impact between the types of intervention, in particular the greater success of personalized messages, implies that it is the personal and face-to-face basis of influence that has an effect, rather than the types of message received and the simple provision of information. This finding suggests the nudge needs to be personal to work.

### What is the intervention?

So far, most Get Out the Vote experiments have been carried out in the United States, which means that, even with its variety of groups and locations, it is not possible to draw conclusions about interventions in the UK context. For a greater degree of universality, interventions in non-US research sites can ascertain whether the impacts of voter mobilization interventions may be generalized comparatively. In addition, they can appraise the strength of effects discovered in the United States, and find out the extent to which context matters in the efficacy of Get Out the Vote campaigns. In this chapter we report on an experiment implemented in the campaign period before the UK General Election of 5 May 2005, which compared door-to-door and telephone canvassing using the same study design (see John and Brannan 2008).

We opted for Wythenshawe and Sale East in Manchester, which had a turnout in the 2001 General Election of 48.6 per cent, much lower than the national average of 59.4 per cent. It also had a very safe majority for the sitting Labour Member of Parliament, which protected us from any allegation of seeking to influence the outcome – as well as the level of turnout – of the election in that constituency. On the other hand, a safe seat presents its own problems because, from a short-term perspective, it is not instrumentally rational for voters to go the polls if the outcome is predetermined, and this privileges justifications based on civic duty rather than those that appeal to the likely impact on outcomes. In practice, we did not find any voters in Wythenshawe who raised this problem directly.

We included in our sample the registered voters for whom we were able to obtain landline telephone numbers. We randomly selected three groups of 2,300 from the 9,976 available for the treatment and control groups. We selected one treatment group to receive the telephone call (the telephone group); the other to receive the visit (the canvassing group). We had no contact with the control group. We sent letters to everyone in the treatment groups to forewarn them of the imminent contact. In the letters we badged ourselves as a university Get Out the Vote campaign; a non-party political group supported by the McDougall Trust, interested in increasing electoral turnout. The letters advised recipients that we would be contacting them to discuss voting and provided contact details to enable recipients to register any concerns.

The door-to-door canvassing was coordinated by the Institute for Political and Economic Governance, a university research institute. The canvassers were predominantly postgraduate students who were enthusiastic about raising electoral turnout, had a good knowledge of the research topic and had an interest in the objectives of the project. As well as offering training and setting up procedures to ensure their safety, we devised a script for the canvassers and callers to work from, which we modified after the pilots for both canvassing and telephoning. This was intended as a guide to be used in a fairly informal conversation, rather than a text to which they should rigidly adhere. In the course of the conversation, which was planned to last up to five minutes, the callers and canvassers were instructed to ask three questions, generally speaking: Do you think voting is important? Do you intend to vote? And will you be voting by post?

However, the main purpose of the conversation was to persuade the citizen to vote, both by providing reasons that it is important and by attempting to respond to any concerns about the voting process. The reasons we provided for the importance of voting are shown in Table 5.1.

**Table 5.1** The script for the telephone and door-to-door canvass

| |
|---|
| It keeps our democratic system working. If not many people voted it could threaten our democracy. Turnout has been falling in recent elections and was only 59 per cent in the last general election. |
| Earlier generations fought for the right to vote and in many countries people are still fighting for that right. |
| Voting gives you a voice and a chance to express your views about issues which affect your life. You *can* influence the outcome and politicians have to listen to communities where more people turn out to vote as their position depends on those people. |
| Voting is easy to do. It doesn't take much time or effort but it is your chance to make a difference. |

For twelve days over the two weeks prior to the General Election, canvassers knocked on doors, following pre-assigned routes around the sample addresses in the constituency. They conducted brief conversations with named contacts when they attempted to persuade them of the merits of voting. The results were recorded on the sheets we provided. Time and resources permitting, the team carried out repeat visits if the initial attempted contact had been unsuccessful.

The telephone calls were conducted by a local survey company, Vision TwentyOne, and took place between 20 and 27 April 2005. The callers used the same script as the canvassers, thus enabling a comparison of the impact of each method. They made up to two repeat calls with a response rate of 47.8 per cent. Turning now to the telephone interviews, there was a lower response rate of 43 per cent was caused by fewer people being available or answering, as well as a higher number refusing to participate (see Figure 5.1).

**Figure 5.1** Responses to door-to-door and telephone canvassing

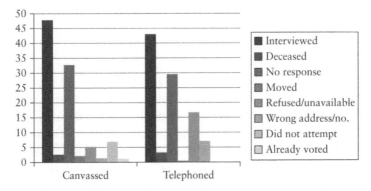

## What did we find?

After removing postal voters and registered deceased from the three groups, checking the official marked electoral registers yielded the turnout rates for control and treatments groups, reported for canvassing in Figure 5.1.

**Figure 5.2** Voter turnout rates in Wythenshawe after the intervention (%)

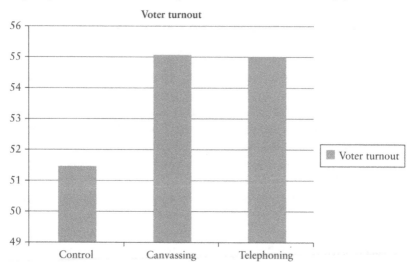

The voter turnout figure in the non-contacted canvassing treatment group is slightly lower than the control group, which is a slight contrast to the telephone group and to US studies which have turnout at the same rates. This difference does not affect the estimation of the treatment effect because of the procedure we adopt for its calculation.

When turning to the difference between the voting rates of the treatment and control groups, as shown in Figure 5.2, as expected we find differences from the interventions: turnout is 55.1 per cent in the canvassed group, 3.6 per cent higher than the control group at 51.5 per cent; and there was turnout of 55 per cent for telephoning, a similar figure of 3.5 per cent higher than turnout in the control group. This figure is known as the 'intent to treat' effect. We cannot, however, make inferences about the impact of the interventions from these figures because they contain electors whom we were unable to contact. To calculate the treatment effect, we report the calculations from a well-known procedure elaborated by Gerber and colleagues (Gerber and Green 2000) who subtract the turnout rate of the control group from that of the treatment group, then divide by the contact rate. This estimates the effect of the canvassing to be 6.7 per cent and for telephoning of 7.3 per cent. Overall the experiment was a success as both interventions had positive, strong and statistically significant impacts, as well as the effective implementation of the two campaigns. The treatment effect of 6.7 per cent from canvassing is in the same margins as the US studies; but the effect of 7.3 per cent from telephoning is in excess of Gerber and Green's original negligible estimates. However, more recent studies produce higher estimates closer to ours. Nickerson revises the expectations of telephoning in the Gerber and Green research by drawing attention to its extensive use in the commercial sector and the opportunities for volunteer telephone banks (Nickerson 2006). Nickerson carried out a series of experiments using volunteer telephoning that involved personalized, chatty and informal calls, producing an average treatment effect of 3.8 per cent. Although Nickerson concludes by saying that on average 'volunteer phone calls are roughly half as effective as face-to-face meetings', the range of treatment effects is between 0.5 and 9.3 per cent, which puts the UK experiment within the upper range. In addition, our results have large standard errors because of relatively small sample sizes, which also place the estimates closer to those in the US. Nonetheless, the impact of telephoning is still high and also comparable with our canvassing effect. This experiment in the UK 2005 General Election is a successful replication of the field experiment method pioneered by Gerber and Green, both in its practical implementation and its results.

It might be argued that such effects are short-lived, but it is possible that voters who are mobilized by a campaign continue to turn out in a subsequent election. It thereby tests the extent to which they gain the habit of voting (Gerber, Green and and Shachar 2003). The research (Cutts, Fieldhouse and John 2009) examined electoral registers for these voters in Wythenshawe for the 2006 English local elections. Descriptive statistics show that the downstream effect of the treatment was quite small at 3 per cent in 2006. But the habit effect was large. Voting in 2005 raised the probability of voting in 2006 by more than half. Regression analysis confirms the size of the habit effect. This is an important finding and shows that the effect of nudge is not just one-off, but continues into the future as citizens get into the habit of acting pro-socially.

## What is the lesson?

The lesson of the 2005 experiment and its follow up, as well as that of more than 200 voter mobilization experiments done in the United States (Green and Gerber 2008), is that light-touch contacts with the citizens can have treatment effects of between 3 and 7 per cent, depending on the context and the type of intervention. That is, simply on the basis of a phone call or a conversation on the door step, citizens can carry out the public-spirited act of voting, which is at low-cost to them, but reinforces the wider role they have as citizens. The effects are relatively modest, but the cost is low, making it an effective nudge form of intervention. In fact, canvassing may be just one among many ways to mobilize citizens: interventions that apply social pressure by informing neighbours of each other's turnout will increase the effect of treatments quite considerably (Gerber *et al.* 2008). We investigate some of these interventions in the next chapter when translated into e-petitions and donations.

The message of this chapter is that the nudge clearly works when getting citizens to participate more. The idea is that providing a cue to the citizens that reminds them of their civic duty can have an impact on their behaviour. There is also a downstream effect of about 50 per cent which shows it is long lasting. The intervention we describe in this chapter is not costly: organizing a door-knock and measuring the impact cost about £18,000. But the effect of this light-touch intervention is not trivial as it can raise voter turnout by about 7n per cent. The implication of these findings is that it does not take much to alter political participation, and it may be done through changing the type of contacts between the state and the citizens in the form of making personal contacts. The nudge can mobilize citizens in positive ways.

*Further reading*

The best review of Get Out the Vote experiments is Green, D.P. and Gerber, A.S. (2008), *Get Out The Vote!: How to Increase Voter Turnout*, 2nd ed., Washington, DC: Brookings Institution Press. The classic research paper is Gerber, A. S. and Green, D.P. (2000), 'The Effects of Canvassing, Telephone Calls, and Direct Mail on Voter Turnout: a Field Experiment', *American Political Science Review*, 94: 653–63. More detail about how to run a voter turnout experiment is contained in John, P. and Brannan, T. (2006), 'How to Mobilise the Electorate: Lessons from the University of Manchester "Get Out the Vote" Experiment', *Representation*, 42: 209–21.

# 6

# Petitioning

## Why study petitioning?

In the last chapter we reviewed some traditional ways of mobilizing citizens through the door-to-door knock or a telephone call. Even though traditional methods remain important, as the prominence of the TV debates in the 2010 General Election campaign show, new forms of communication are emerging though the use of personal information technology devices and the 24-hour availability of the internet. These are going to become more common ways of carrying out business, will be linked to community action and will be a natural route for people to get involved in politics. Now that the internet is at the heart of political mobilization and is powerful because of its ability to provide real-time feedback about what other people are doing, it may produce a kind of social pressure that encourages people to participate (Lupia and Sin 2003). Lupia and Sin argue that the internet might scale up this kind of social incentive, while minimizing the cost.

In terms of politics and social action, the internet reduces the costs of participation and so should make participation an easier and more frequent occurrence. It also means that, given the large amount of information to which individuals are likely to be susceptible, the way in which information is presented may provide an opportunity for nudge. The relevant aspect of the internet is that information can be manipulated by the way it is presented on-screen. There are also technical features of the internet which allow for real-time feedback that is very hard to achieve in the offline world. This can be set up to promote interactions between citizens, for example for the purposes of deliberation, which we examine in Chapter 9. The irony this chapter seeks to confront is that, while deliberative democrats have seen the internet as a potential for citizen mobilization, in fact it may be better able to deliver discrete nudges to mobilize citizens.

From the policy-maker's point of view, there is an additional argument. The traditional forms of mobilizing are complicated to organize. It is also hard to work out what it is about mobilizing that works – is it the provision of information, or is it the personal contact, or is it persuasion? The argument of this chapter is that through the internet, where information technology is very close and in everyday reach of most citizens there is an opportunity to reach out to many more citizens than by face-to-face methods.

In this experiment we test this hypothesis by examining the social incentives which are at work when people are deciding whether to participate in something. Specifically, we look at how individuals use information about the participation of others as a way of making their decision about whether to participate or not. When such participation takes place online, there is a far greater possibility of the potential participant receiving real-time feedback information about how many other people have participated and this is something that someone who signs a petition in the street, or throws money into a charity collector's bucket, is unlikely to receive. Furthermore, new types of social information become available through recommendation systems (as used by Amazon to tell people about other preferences of people who have bought a certain book), reputation systems (as used by eBay to rate the trustworthiness of participants) and user feedback applications. Such applications are most prevalent in the private sector, but have high potential to be applied to political and social activity. The internet, therefore, changes the information environment in which people decide to participate (Benkler 2006; Bimber 2003).

We report on a laboratory-based and a quasi-field experiment to investigate the effect of social information in this changed environment. In both experiments, subjects were asked to sign petitions and to donate a small proportion of their turn-up fee to the cause of the petition. The experiments investigated whether seeing the numbers of other people signing (as opposed to not seeing that) influenced the willingness to sign and contribute, how the actual number of other people participating influences willingness to contribute, and the direction of that influence.

## What do we already know?

Experiments provide the best way to evaluate how different kinds of social information affect participation, as the treatments can be manipulations of the kind of information on offer, something that is highly tractable with current internet technology although there is little other experimental work tackling this question. The main example is the experiments of Best, Krueger and Ladewig that show that the public perceives online activities (such as volunteering time, donating money and signing a petition) to be riskier (in terms of an adverse consequence such as stolen personal information arising) than comparable offline ones, suggesting this as an explanation for low levels of online participation in comparison to offline environments and contrary to the hopes of some observers (Best, Krueger and Ladewig 2007: 15). Similarly, Oostveen and van den Besselaar report experiments that test the impact on voting behaviour of the perceived security of electronic voting systems, showing that the more trusted and secure a voter perceived a technology to be, the more likely they were to vote more radically (Oostveen and van den Besselaar 2004; Oostveen and van den Besselaar 2006). Xenos and Kyoung carried out a controlled test of the effects of youth-oriented political portals, finding only weak effects for exposure to such portals on self-reported cognitive engagement with election information (Xenos and Kyoung 2008). But in general there is little experimental work looking at social information effects on online mobilization around public goods.

## What was the intervention?

The purpose of our experiments is to test how social information provided via the internet affects collective action. Does such information result in social pressure and is such social pressure maximized when numbers are small (so that an individual feels their action to be more noticeable) or large (so that an individual feels more bombarded with social pressure and other social incentives)? Our expectation is that information about the preferences of others will affect people's decision whether to incur costs in the pursuit of collective action. If people know (for example) how many people have signed a petition, we hypothesize that it will affect their willingness to sign or to incur other costs in the pursuit of the petitioned issue. We believe that in the earliest stage of a petition, there would be a very rapid joining in response to feedback information, as people would feel that their contribution would make a difference. In the later stages of the petition, we would then expect the information to have little – or even a negative – effect, as people would feel that their participation would not make much difference. At a certain point, when critical mass is reached, the information would again have a dramatically positive effect because high numbers of other signatories would exert a social pressure on individuals to sign.

The experiments tested these hypotheses by exploring the effect of being given information about the mobilization of others on any one individual subject's willingness to incur costs in supporting a collective issue. In the first lab-based experiment, 47 individuals were randomly recruited from OxLab's subject database (which includes both students and non-students from the city of Oxford). We provided both groups with a list of six petitions that were active at the time of the experiment on the website of the Prime Minister (http://petitions.number10.gov.uk) and asked, first, whether they agreed with the issues being petitioned for; second, they were asked to browse the internet during ten minutes in order to inform themselves about the given petition's issue; and third, they were queried whether they (a) would sign the petition on the issue and (b) whether they would donate a small proportion of their participation fee towards supporting the issue (or against the petition if they declined to sign it). Participants were divided into two groups: individuals assigned to the treatment group received information about how many people had signed the petition (petitions had varying numbers of signatories – data were drawn from real petitions so there was no deception involved) whereas subjects in the control group received no such information.

As we sourced the petitions from the No. 10 Downing Street website, access to it was blocked during the experiment to prevent those in the second treatment from finding this information. Subjects provided socio-demographic information, attitudes, perceptions of the experiment and levels of internet ability in a post-experiment questionnaire. Subjects were incentivized to participate by a payment of between £12 and £15, depending upon the amount they chose to donate to the various causes. All subject information was fully anonymized and no addresses were collected.

Participants were asked to consider six petitions. These addressed the following issues (the number of signatories provided to the treatment group is shown in brackets):

1. To introduce a tax on plastic carrier bags (665,768).
2. To exert pressure on the Japanese government to halt its programme of whaling (9).
3. To create a new public holiday, the National Day of Remembrance (369,492).
4. To provide free prescriptions for asthma sufferers, unrelated to income (11).
5. To employ a policy of an opt-out system (instead of opt-in) for organ donation (1,234,117).
6. To scrap the introduction of compulsory identity cards (6).

In order to avoid using deception in the experiment, subjects were presented with existing petitions and their actual numbers of signatories. Subjects did not actually sign the petitions during the experiment, but were provided with the opportunity to do so after its completion. All the money raised by the subjects during the experiment was donated to the respective causes by the research team after the experiment.

The quasi-field experiment used a larger subject pool: 668 people, contacted and recruited from OxLab's subject database, who participated in the experiment remotely using their own internet connection. Through a web interface we designed, participants were asked to consider six issues successively and for each: (a) to express their willingness to sign a petition supporting the issue; and (b) to donate a small amount of their participation fee to supporting the issue (or against the petition if they declined to sign it). In order to sign a petition subjects were required to provide name, email and address. While they did not really sign the petition this meant they had to incur some costs to support their statement. Participants could donate 20p towards every issue and the sum was then doubled by the experimenters. Subjects were randomly allocated across a control group (of 173) and a treatment group (of 495). All participants received the same six petitions but carrying different social information. In the control group, participants received no information about other people signing. In the treatment groups, subjects were shown two petitions in each of the following categories:

1. Petitions with a very large numbers of signatories (S > 1 million);
2. Petitions with a medium numbers of signatories (100 < S < 1 million);
3. Petitions with very low numbers of signatories (S < 100).

The sub-treatment groups were as follows:

Group B (164) received two 'low-numbered' petitions, two 'high' and two 'middle';

Group C (171) received two 'middle-numbered' petitions, two 'low' and two 'high';

Group D (160) received two 'high-numbered' petitions, two 'middle' and two 'low'.

In order to eliminate systematic biases of individual petitions the order in which participants were presented with the six petitions was randomized.

We incentivized the participants with a small payment (£6–£8), which varied according to the amount they chose to donate, which we paid with Amazon.co.uk vouchers. There was a pre-experiment questionnaire to establish the extent to which participants agreed (or not) with the issues in the petitions. Again, we anonymized all subject information and did not collect addresses. The petitions were as follows (with the high, medium and low numbers provided shown in brackets):

1. National governments should put pressure on the Chinese leadership to show restraint and respect for human rights in response to protests in Tibet (High: 1,682,242, Medium: 1,189, Low: 76).
2. National governments should negotiate and adopt a treaty to ban the use of cluster bombs (High: 1,200,000, Medium: 330,000, Low: 7).

3. Governments should lobby the Japanese government to stop commercial whaling of the Humpback whale (High: 1,082,808, Medium: 57,299, Low: 98).

4. Governments should support a stronger multinational force to protect the people of the Darfur region of Sudan (High: 1,001,012, Medium: 5,978, Low: 16).

5. World leaders should negotiate a global deal on climate change (High: 2,600,053, Medium: 575,000, Low: 53).

6. Governments should work to negotiate new trade rules – fair rules to make a real difference in the fight against poverty (High: 17,800,244; Medium: 22,777, Low, 25).

Again, there was no deception. The petitions were shown in generic format (to control for the reputation effect that different web platforms would bring), yet the numbers of signatories shown to the participants were taken from existing online petitions that had been created on these issues with different numbers of signatories (low, medium and high). The issues were all selected to be of international significance and petitions used were all drawn from across different geographical spaces and points in time (during the last three years). Again, subjects did not actually sign the petitions in the experiment, but at the end of the experiment the interface directed them to a site where they could. The research team made the donations to the causes when the experiment finished.

## What did we find?

As there were six petitions in both laboratory and field, we stacked the data so as to examine the variation according to the numbers of signatories that subjects could see before signing, which yielded a total of 282 person-petitions for the laboratory and 4,008 for the field. In the initial lab-based experiment, we found that 59 per cent of petitions were signed overall: 54 per cent in the control group and 63 per cent of the treatment group (those who received information about other people signing), indicating a 9 per cent point different between the treatment and control groups. We identified one issue (out of six) where subjects were significantly more likely to sign a petition if they received information that many other people had signed than if they received no information. This petition was the one supporting an opt-out system for kidney donation, the only one for which the number of signatures was over a million (1,234,117), suggesting a possible hypothesis that the threshold at which social information makes a difference could be one million. Across the six petitions there was a positive correlation with the number of other signatories (for high numbers) and an individual's likelihood of signing. The numbers of subjects were too small to come to firm conclusions about the distribution of effects on people's likelihood to participate. But the identification of a distinct effect for high numbers on the propensity to sign and a weaker effect of medium numbers on propensity to donate (see below) fed into the design of the larger quasi-field experiment.

For the quasi-field experiment, 61.5 per cent of the petitions presented to the control group were signed. Of the petitions presented with low numbers, slightly less (-0.9 per cent) were signed and for those presented with medium numbers, slightly more (+1.9 per cent) were signed. For those presented with high numbers, 66.7 per cent were signed (that is, 5.2 per cent more than in the control group) and this result is statistically significant. The percentage of participants signing each petition is shown in Figure 6.1, compared with the proportion of people signing in the control group (shown as the baseline). The figure shows clearly that for all petitions, high numbers had a positive effect. This is statistically significant for the climate change and fair trade petitions. This effect was strongest for the petition on fair trade, which also had by far the highest number of signatories in this category (17.8 million), leading to a possible hypothesis that the effect of high numbers varied according to the magnitude of the number of other signatures. But when we tested this hypothesis we found no effect.

A stronger test for the actual willingness of a subject to support a petition is whether or not the subject would also commit to a donation. This would cost the subject real money and was a chance to put their money where their mouth is. On average two-thirds of those who signed a petition went on to make a donation. Interestingly, an as yet unexplained feature of the patterns of donation is that for each petition in the larger experiment, almost exactly two-thirds of those who signed went on to donate, suggesting a general relationship. Even with the rather different experimental set-up and much smaller numbers in the laboratory experiment, a similar effect could be observed. But here the effect of the numbers was less clear, but low numbers had a negative effect in most cases except the petitions on whaling and on Darfur, and high numbers had a small positive effect in all but one (the petition on cluster bombs). The difference between signing and donations is interesting, possibly due to the fact that less people donate than sign (40 per cent versus 63 per cent). It seems that these individuals have a higher threshold for donating and are consequently less influenced by high numbers and more easily discouraged from doing so by low numbers of other signatories.

**Figure 6.1** Subjects signing petitions in field experiment (by number of other signatories)

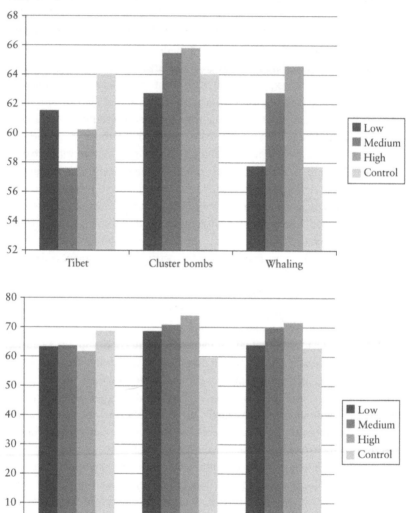

## What is the lesson?

The results indicate we have found evidence that Olson's claims about social pressure in small groups could be extended in a low-cost way to large groups. Internet-enabled social information remodels the cost benefit equation of political participation. While internet research abounds with claims of how the internet enhances political participation, empirical evidence is scarce. These results provide insight into the influence of one type of social information – the raw numbers of other people participating – but there is potential for further investigation into the influence of other types of social information. In our experiments, subjects could only see the raw numbers of other people currently participating, rather than any information about the personality of other participants, their socio-demographic status, or their experience of past participation. Newer features of the internet allow the provision of these other types of information, particularly those associated with so-called Web 2.0 technologies based on user-generated content, which include recommendation systems, reputation systems, blogs, user feedback applications, video-sharing sites and discussion streams such as Twitter. When used for political activity, these applications allow participants to see many other types of social information. For example, they can see other participants' comments and feedback in real time and information about how people similar to them in terms of preferences have behaved. They can see what other participants are willing to pledge, if other people also participate (see http://www.pledgebank.org). These types of social information are likely to have an even greater and more complex effect on political participation. The experiments reported here should be helpful in providing a pointer for future study of the implications of these other types of social information.

This kind of information could also inform the design of participatory initiatives, in terms of when it is good to give information and when it is not. In designing the experiment, we found a huge range of online petitions set up by non-governmental organizations and individuals, some of which gave no information at all about how many people had participated and some of which gave full information. Our findings suggest that there are circumstances where it makes sense to withhold such information (when numbers are below a million) and circumstances where it makes sense to provide it (when numbers are higher than one million), as well as circumstances where it makes no difference.

The phenomena noted in the opening paragraph of this article point to the changing scope and nature of mass mobilization, for example in terms of size and geographical reach and demographic make-up. We do not make any claims about the effectiveness of these mobilizations. But the significance of these mobilizations remains as an indication of a changed environment for political participation. Understanding this changed world will be a key challenge for political science in the future. In the United States, for example, the 2008 election of Barack Obama was massively affected by the cumulation of millions of small-scale activities (such as video-sharing, micro-participation in the campaign and individual donations) with readily available information about these activities (such as video downloads, activities undertaken and donations made) shaping patterns of participation. Such an increase in political participation is enabled by the vast reach of internet. In this way, these experiments show the importance of the increasing automation of political activity and the capacity of the internet to provide real-time information about the participation of others.

This chapter and the previous one show that it is difficult to adjudicate between older mechanisms of personal contact and newer ones using new technology. Both are nudge and both work in our examples, with a similar magnitude of effects. But they can be distinguished. The internet nudges are much easier to achieve since they make use of an easier way to provide information than identifying and locating a citizen and approaching them individually with the information. As with other aspects of political participation – and the experiments on mobilizing it – there is an element of self-selection, but it seems internet nudges win out.

*Further reading*

For a general account of the internet and political engagement see Bimber, B. (2003), *Information and American Democracy: Technology in the Evolution of Political Power*, Cambridge: Cambridge University Press. Dunleavy, P., Margetts, H., Bastow, S. and Tinkler, J. (2006), *Digital Era Governance: IT Corporations, the State, and E-government*, Oxford: Oxford University Press, provides an argument about the benefits of e-government and how best to improve contacts between the citizens and the state. The best summary of the collective action issues raised by the internet is Lupia, A. and Sin, G. (2003), 'Which Public Goods are Endangered? How Evolving Communication Technologies Affect the Logic of Collective Action', *Public Choice*, 117: 315–31.

# Giving

## Why study charitable giving?

The situations in which citizens are asked to give are numerous and varied: theatregoers are asked to sponsor a seat, parents are asked by schools to give up time to help with the summer fete and charities seek donations of money or used goods. It seems that many organizations are on the lookout for the best ways to persuade citizens to donate time, money or other personal resources that assist the public good. Many of these examples are not controversial, but rather are widely accepted as the right thing to do: most people like to be the kind of person who gives money to charity, gives time to the local school or helps others less fortunate than themselves. But despite good intentions, citizens are busy people, easily distracted, with many other priorities, and so there are many missed opportunities to give.

In this chapter we consider ways in which nudges can persuade citizens to give time, money or other things for wider public benefit. This chapter starts by looking briefly at the current state of the evidence on what might encourage people to give, and in particular we focus on two methods that can potentially promote giving: asking someone to make a pledge or commitment that they will later make a donation; and offering public recognition as a thank you for a donation. We describe a randomized controlled trial which tests the impact of asking for a pledge and offering public recognition on donations of books for schools in South Africa, and we review the lessons of the experiment for nudges.

## What do we know about how to encourage giving?

A web of complex and overlapping issues can impact on what might encourage people to give to charitable causes or to help others. We can learn much about what leads to altruism from economics and psychology research. Motives can be divided into three broad categories: intrinsic motivation, such as pure altruism or moral preferences; extrinsic motivation, including material rewards and benefits gained by giving; and image motivation, the chance to signal to others that one is good (Ariely, Bracha and Meier 2009). In a similar vein, a strong factor in encouraging altruism is caring about the situation of others: caring can be induced by empathy with the charity recipient and can also arise from moral beliefs. While caring about others is an important push towards giving, donors are influenced by other, less altruistic motives too, and may be dissuaded from giving, for example if to do so goes against the trends in their social group, if they lack the necessary resources or if they just do not have the opportunity due to situational constraints or lack of awareness (Farsides 2007). People are more likely to donate if they are told beforehand that another donor has already made a substantial contribution (signalling that this is a trustworthy charity to donate to) (Huck and Rasul 2008) or that any contribution they make will be matched from another source (Huck and Rasul 2008).

## Pledging to give

One way of encouraging giving is to ask for a pledge. Practical examples of how this method is already used to promote giving include the growing number of pledge schemes that have emerged in recent years. Pledge schemes are set up by government or non-governmental organizations to invite individuals to make a public commitment to a behaviour change. Amnesty International's global campaign against violence towards women includes a series of pledge-signing events, where people pledge not to remain silent about abuse. Citizens can pledge to become more globally aware and speak up for the disadvantaged in the Global Citizen Campaign. There are a number of environmental pledge schemes, usually web-based, where individuals can sign up to one or more sustainable behaviours. Other examples are the use of pledges as part of protest campaigns, pledges to be vegetarian and local schemes like Chorley Smile, where residents of Chorley, northwest England, are asked by their local council to sign up to do things that will benefit their town.

Research from psychology suggests that in certain circumstances people who pledge are likely to act on their good intention. Consistency is an important character trait, with people who behave inconsistently being widely regarded as unreliable and untrustworthy. There is a strong internal and societal pressure on individuals to behave in a way that is consistent with how they see themselves. Individuals who make a pledge to behave in a certain way can start to see themselves in a way that is consistent with that behaviour, leading to long-term change in their attitudes and behaviour. The commitment can act as a catalyst, providing the internal conviction for a new identity and leading to behaviour that corresponds with that conviction, which can last well beyond the duration of the commitment. If an individual gives a commitment that they will volunteer, vote, recycle or not drop litter, it perhaps increases the likelihood that they will later act in a way that is consistent with those attitudes: 'When individuals feel committed to a certain type of behaviour, they will often adopt an identity that is consistent with that behaviour, the result of which frequently is long-lasting behaviour change' (Bator and Cialdini 2000: 536). Their compliance with the original commitment can be enduring, even if they are called upon to act by a different person and some substantial time later (McKenzie-Mohr and Smith 1999). Closely related to pledging are 'foot in the door' techniques: asking people to undertake a small action makes it more likely that they will later agree to a much larger request. Doing the initial small action causes the person to think of themselves as 'the kind of person who does this sort of thing, who agrees to requests by strangers, who takes action on things he believes in, who cooperates with good causes' (Freedman and Fraser 1966: 201).

Field research on whether pledging does lead to behaviour change is somewhat inconclusive. A number of studies have found that asking people to pledge can raise recycling rates, and it will raise recycling at a similar rate to other alternative approaches such as incentives or persuasion (Reams and Ray 1993: Burn and Oskamp 1996; Katzev and Pardini 1987; Bryce *et al.* 1997), but it is not clear whether it is the personal contact with the household or the pledging that changes behaviour. A more recent report compared canvassing campaigns with and without pledges and found that the pledge made no significant difference (Thomas 2006). Pledges are often sought as part of a wider promotional campaign (see for example Ludwig, Buchholz and Clarke 2005 on getting cyclists to wear helmets and Geller, Kalsher, Rudd and Lehman 1989 on getting car drivers to wear safety belts), making it hard to distinguish whether it is the pledge or the wider campaign that gets people to change their behaviour. Asking for a prediction of whether they would vote increased the propensity of students to register to vote and then turn out to vote, compared to a control group (Greenwald *et al.* 1987), but a larger scale replication study, among a broader cross-section of US residents, found that asking for a prediction had no significant effect on voting behaviour (Smith *et al.* 2003). The likelihood of a pledge leading to long-lasting change will vary according to the nature of the pledge: change is more likely if the commitment is voluntary, made in public and relates to an issue the pledger is already concerned about.

## Public recognition of giving

Another way of encouraging people to give is to promise them public recognition as a thank you for making a donation. Practical examples of how public recognition include the inclusion of the names of donor individuals and companies in brochures for public festivals and charitable events, and prominent public displays of lists of sponsors in art galleries, theatres and community centres. Laboratory experiments indicate that donors appreciate the prestige they get from having their donations made public, and when donations are advertised in categories (for example, gold, silver or bronze donors), people will more often give the minimum amount needed to appear in a higher category (Harburgh 1998).

Image motivation describes how citizens may be motivated by how others perceive their behaviour: when individuals are seeking social approval, they may choose to exhibit qualities that they think are widely regarded as good. Ariely *et al.* write 'People will act more pro-socially in the public sphere than in private settings' (Ariely *et al.* 2009: 544). A recent laboratory experiment found that people were more likely to contribute to charity if their donation was made public and these results were partially sustained in a field experiment, in which people were more likely to cycle on an exercise bike for charity if the bike was placed in a prominent public position. Interestingly, the study found that when it is made clear that there are monetary incentives to be accrued from behaving pro-socially, people are deterred from making public donations (because the signal it gives is no longer so purely altruistic) but there is not the same crowding-out effect on private donations (Ariely *et al.* 2009). Get Out the Vote experiments have found that 'social pressure' mailings can increase voter turnout, either by letting people know whether or not they or their neighbours voted last time, inducing shame that their behaviour is observable to others (Gerber *et al.* 2008) or by simply thanking people for voting in a previous election (Panagopoulos 2010).

### What was the intervention?

We undertook a randomized controlled trial to test the effectiveness of these two nudges – asking for a pledge and offering public recognition – on charitable donations (see Cotterill, John and Richardson 2010). We were interested to discover whether making a pledge encourages people to give: whether those who are invited to make a pledge are more likely to later donate a book, because they feel they have made a promise and want to see it through. We were also interested in whether households who are advised their donation will be made public are encouraged to give because their generosity will be advertised to their peers. In the spring of 2010 we organized a campaign to collect books for use in school libraries in South Africa. The research was undertaken in partnership with Community HEART, a UK registered charity formed by anti-apartheid activist Denis Goldberg, which supports local self-help initiatives in South Africa (registered charity number 1052817). Community HEART collects children's books in the UK and transports them to South Africa, where they are used to set up school libraries (http://www.community-heart.org.uk/projects/books/books.htm)

## Population and randomization

The research was undertaken with 12,000 households in two electoral wards in Manchester, UK. One of the wards is relatively affluent and largely made up of private housing; the other is relatively deprived, with a high proportion of social rented housing. All residential properties in those two areas, both houses and flats, were included in the study. Households were randomly assigned to one of three groups of equal size: a pledge group; a pledge and publicity group; and a control group.

## Intervention – a campaign for book donations

Each of the 12,000 households were sent two letters about an upcoming Children's Book Week, asking them to donate a second-hand book to help set up school libraries in South Africa. The letters were of a very simple design, on University of Manchester letterhead paper, addressed to 'The Residents'. The letters contained the same common message:

Children's Book Week
Sat 27th February–Saturday 6th March 2010
Please donate a second hand book
(in good condition, for a child of any age)
Manchester residents are being asked to donate a book to help set up school libraries in South Africa. Millions of children in South Africa have no books and we can help by donating books we no longer want. The children's book collection is being organized by Manchester University together with Community HEART. Community HEART is a UK registered charity which supports local self-help initiatives in South Africa (registered charity no. 1052817). They collect children's books in the UK and transport them to South Africa, where they are used to set up school libraries.

After this common message, the wording of the letter was different, depending on what group the household had been allocated to:

1. Pledge group. In the first letter we asked households to 'Please pledge to donate a second hand book' by postcard, email or phone, and we enclosed a pledge card. Regardless of whether or not they returned a pledge, a few weeks later we sent a reminder letter, with details of drop-off points.
2. Pledge and publicity group. We sent two similar letters, asking for a pledge, and in addition told households that 'A list of everyone who donates a book will be displayed locally.'
3. Control group. We sent two similar letters, without the pledge or the offer of publicity.

### Outcome measurement

Residents were asked to take donated books to one of six book collection points, three in each area, during Children's Book Week, 27 February–6 March 2010. We chose a variety of different drop-off points, in various locations, including two libraries, a primary school, a children's centre, a cafe and a community centre. Residents were sent a bag to use for their donated books and each bag had a unique identifier number to allow us to track who had already given a book. Donors could choose to write their name on the bag, or to donate anonymously. We collected the book bags from the drop-off points and for each donation we recorded the donor address, the number of books donated and the chosen drop-off point. Afterwards, to thank donors, we displayed a poster with the results and the names of book donors (excluding anonymous donors) in all the local collection points.

### Were the nudges successful?

The overall response was much higher than we anticipated: a total of 7,000 books were donated. The books were very high quality and included books for all ages of children. 7.2 per cent of the control group gave books, compared to 8.1 per cent of the pledge group and 8.8 per cent of the pledge and publicity group (Figure 7.1).

The response from the pledge group (8.1 per cent of households) was higher than the control group, but the treatment effect was not statistically significant. We can conclude that asking for the pledge on its own possibly has a very small effect on donations, but does not lead to a significant increase the number of donations. But the combined approach of asking for a pledge and at the same time offering local publicity did lead to a substantial rise in donations and the difference was statistically significant. The difference between the control group (7.2 per cent of households gave books) and the pledge and publicity group (8.8 per cent of households gave books) is 1.6 per cent.

**Figure 7.1** Percentage of households donating books from each treatment group

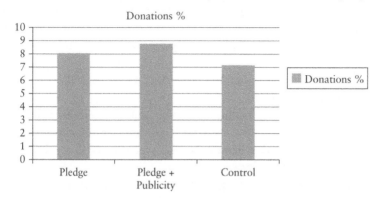

The response to the book collection was highest in less deprived neighbourhoods; in areas with a high proportion of retired residents; and in areas with a low proportion of single-person households. After taking those into account, the effect of an area having high numbers of children under 16 or a high number of religious people was not statistically significant.

A pledge and publicity campaign could potentially be applied to other situations where citizens are encouraged to adopt civic behaviour. Examples might include:

1. a pledge to undertake environmental action such as recycling, energy saving, or alternatives to car travel, followed by publicity for those who stick to the pledge;
2. a pledge to volunteer or campaign for a cause, with a promise that a list will be displayed as a thank you to those who gave their time;
3. at the neighbourhood level, a pledge to keep to tenancy agreements followed by publicity for those who stick to it;
4. a pledge to attend an annual workplace blood donation session, with a thank you list of donors displayed afterwards.

The book collection experiment has several implications for a nudge strategy. It is a widely held view in behavioural economics (Dawney and Shah 2005), social psychology (Cialdini 2009) and social marketing (McKenzie-Mohr and Smith 1999) that asking for a pledge increases the likelihood that individuals will later give. This is based on the premise that once someone makes a commitment they start to feel like the sort of person that behaves in that way and they don't want to appear inconsistent to themselves or others. As we saw earlier, commitments are thought to work best if they are voluntary, are made in public, relate to an issue the pledger is already concerned about and are requested as part of a wider campaign. Taking each of these in turn, in our book collection experiment:

1. Pledges were voluntary in the sense that there was no pressure or compulsion to pledge.
2. Pledges were made by sending a postcard, email or phone call to a person unknown to them, who works for a university, in the knowledge that it will be recorded. While this is not a pledge made in a public place, neither is it a purely private act.
3. We have no way of knowing whether those who pledged were already concerned about the plight of children's education in South Africa. But in the absence of any pressure to pledge, we might assume that those who pledged were either committed to the cause or were interested in off-loading used books. Certainly, many of those who pledged expressed strong sentiments towards the topic.
4. Resource constraints and the need to maintain experimental conditions prevented us mounting a significant campaign. However, as well as posting two letters on the book campaign to each household, posters advertising the collection were displayed in the six drop-off points, and the campaign was branded as part of Children's Book Week 2010.

In this book collection experiment, we found that asking for a pledge did not lead to a significant rise in book donations, over and above a general request letter. A pledge campaign of the sort we organized is not an effective way to boost charitable donations. This finding seems to counter the prevailing view.

The focus of our experiment is on whether pledge schemes are an effective tool to use to encourage civic behaviour, rather than whether people who pledge are more likely to give. Our research did show that there is a high correlation between pledging and taking action; more than two-thirds of those who pledged went on to make a book donation. However, this simple observation that those who pledge often go on to give cannot shed much light on the relationship between pledging and giving, because if we only look at the behaviour of pledgers, without a control group, it is hard to know whether it is the pledge that makes them do it or just their disposition. It is likely that the sort of people who go to the effort of making a pledge are more disposed than others to go to a local drop-off point to donate a book.

Citizens do not act is isolation; our actions are influenced by what others do, what we think is expected of us and how we want to be viewed by others. In particular, we care about the views of our peers. The promise of information disclosure can have a powerful effect in promoting civic behaviour, by signalling that the actions of an individual will be made known more widely (Thaler and Sunstein 2008). Research shows that people want to be thanked when they participate (Rogers 2004). Too often people do not get thanked for the good things they do in life. In the book collection experiment, the most effective request was to ask people to pledge and to tell them their name would be posted locally, as a thank you for their donation. The combination of pledge and publicity raised book donations by almost a quarter, from 7 per cent to 9 per cent of households. Asking people for a pledge does not work on its own: it is the pledge and the promise of publicity that together have the big impact on behaviour. Our research shows that people can be spurred on to help others by the promise that their actions will be made public.

The response to the book collection was overwhelming: a very simple letter from a stranger on behalf of a small unknown charity to help children in a foreign country caused 1,000 people to donate a total of 7,000 books. Some people purchased new books; others gave their treasured childhood possessions including school prizes; young children were encouraged by parents to donate; up to a dozen people went on to organize their own collections in schools, nurseries and workplaces. This demonstrates the power of a simple request: even without the pledge or the promise of publicity 7 per cent of those who were asked chose to give. We already know that being asked to participate is a key driver of pro-social behaviour. The request is most effective if it comes from a family member or friend, but employers and faith organizations can be important mobilizers. Although it is likely that people will respond more enthusiastically to an invitation from someone close to them, mobilization by a local authority can be effective: the invitation both informs the citizen of an opportunity of which they may not otherwise have been aware and conveys that the authority values their opinion (Lowndes *et al.* 2006; Rogers 2004).

*Further reading*
The key text on influence is Cialdini, R.B. (2009), *Influence: Science and Practice*, Needham Heights, MA: Allyn and Bacon (see Chapter Three,

'Commitment and Consistency: Hobgoblins of the Mind'. Also useful is McKenzie-Mohr, D. and Smith, W. (1999), *Fostering Sustainable Behavior: An Introduction to Community-Based Social Marketing*, Gabriola Island, Canada: New Society Publishers (especially Chapter Three, 'Commitment: From Good Intentions to Action').

# 8

# Donating

## Why study organ donation?

A shortage of organ donors in many countries has made the issue of organ donation defaults and registration systems the subject of contemporary international debate. In the UK for instance, only 27 per cent of the population is on the organ donor register. This number falls far short of the level needed to secure enough organs for transplant, with approximately 8,000 people on the waiting list for transplants and 1,000 people having died in 2007/8 whilst on the waiting list (Department of Health 2008). Estimates suggest that a minimum of 50 per cent more organs than are currently available are needed, and the gap between supply and demand is growing by 8 per cent each year (Department of Health 2008). A similar picture is reported in the United States, where in 2002 a total of 6,679 patients died whilst on the waiting list (Abadie and Gay 2006). There is a gap between demand for organs and supply in all EU member states and the gap is increasing in most cases (Eurotransplant 2006).

By joining an organ donor register, a citizen makes a pledge to be a potential donor if their organs can be used for transplantation after they die. The policy perspective is that we need more donors to register in order to ensure that organ supply meets demand. How can we best ask citizens to make a choice about this issue and get donation registration up to levels that will increase the life chances of those many millions who might ultimately benefit from organ transplantation?

In this chapter we begin by discussing different systems for registering organ donors, each with a different default position: the opt-out system, which assumes people are donors unless they actively choose not to be; the opt-in system, where people are assumed not to be donors unless they make a conscious choice to register; and a mandated choice system where no assumption is made about people's preferences but they are required to choose. We then describe two experimental interventions which used a combination of nudge and think techniques to attempt to boost numbers of registrations on the organ donor list.

## Why study organ donation systems of registering?

The system for registering donors is only one factor potentially influencing whether or not people agree to be donors but research suggests that it is an important factor. Registration systems vary across the world and generally fall into one of two camps. In some countries, in order to be considered as donors, citizens must actively make this pledge during their lifetime by opting-in to an organ donor register. Informed consent or opt-in systems, at the time of writing, operate in the UK, the Netherlands, Germany, Denmark, Australia, New Zealand, Japan, Canada and the majority of US states. Citizens are asked to register on a website or by completing a form stating that they would like to become donors, or they are given the option to sign up whilst undertaking other registration processes, for instance passport or driving licence registration. Typically, the wording of the question in an informed consent system asks people whether they would like to become an organ donor and they simply tick the box to join up. The default position is that people are assumed not to be donors.

The other camp is where people must actively opt out if they do not wish to be donors. These are what is called the presumed consent countries and include Israel, Singapore, the Czech Republic, Poland, Bulgaria, Estonia, Hungary, Latvia, Slovenia, France, Belgium, Austria, Italy, Spain, Portugal, Greece, Cyprus, Norway, Finland and Sweden. In these countries, citizens are given the opportunity to opt out through a variety of mechanisms, for instance through an opt-out register, a non-donor card or during driving licence registration. In this case, the default is shifted, and people are assumed to be willing donors unless they state otherwise.

Interest in organ donation defaults is on the increase because the default position appears to matter: presumed consent countries have significantly higher organ donation rates than informed consent countries. In view of this stark contrast, many countries operating informed consent systems have begun to discuss the possibility of changing their default to assume people are donors unless they opt out. In the section below we outline some comparative evidence on organ donor levels in countries with different defaults.

## What do we already know?

Countries where people are assumed to be willing donors unless they opt out achieve organ donation rates around 25–30 per cent higher on average than countries where people are not assumed to be donors (Abadie and Gay 2006). Even when other potentially important factors such as culture, religion and organ donation infrastructure are controlled for, presumed consent legislation has a positive and sizeable effect on organ donation rates (Abadie and Gay 2006; Rithalia, McDaid, Suekarran, Norman, Myers and Sowden 2009). The percentage of citizens actually signed up as donors in those countries operating informed consent systems ranges from 4 to 28 per cent. By contrast, countries with presumed consent systems achieve donor registration rates of between 86 per cent and 100 per cent (Johnson and Goldstein 2003). In presumed consent countries, it would seem that people don't bother opting out. For countries currently operating informed consent systems and seeking to increase their rate of organ donor registration, a change of system could help overcome the organ deficit.

From a behavioural economics perspective, shifting the default position to presumed consent makes sense. As Chapter 1 pointed out, we know that in the absence of strong incentives to change, people have an in-built propensity to maintain the status quo. Behavioural economics says that cognitive limitations lead people to employ shortcuts or heuristics to help in their decision-making. A common heuristic in any decision is to accept the default position if one has been preselected on our behalf. The default position – or status quo – provides the rule of thumb needed when we are faced with decisions that we either want to put off for another time or find difficult to make. Moreover, from a psychological perspective, people are more concerned with losses than with potential gains (Kahneman and Tversky 1979). Where the potential gains or losses of proactively making a choice are unclear, inactivity (that is accepting the default) is often viewed as the most favourable option, costing nothing in time and effort.

Mandated choice, the more neutral alternative, does not operate in many countries and consequently there is limited evidence about the effect of this type of system on organ donor registration rates. However, one online experiment involving 161 participants conducted in the United States (Johnson and Goldstein 2003) investigated opt-in and opt-out defaults as compared to a neutral question with no default. Participants were placed in one of these conditions and asked whether, if moving to a new state, they would give their consent to become a donor. The opt-out condition generated the highest number of hypothetical donors, with 82 per cent saying yes, as compared to 79 per cent in the neutral condition and 43 per cent in the opt-in condition. This study, although based on relatively small numbers, highlights the possibility that a mandated choice system with no default could generate similar numbers of donors to a presumed consent system.

## What is the debate?

Should government provide the nudge and shift choice architecture so that people are assumed to be donors unless they opt out? The main argument for change relates to the need for greater numbers of donors and, as we have already seen, presumed consent legislation appears to be positively associated with higher organ donor registrations. A second argument relates to a major problem in organ transplantation. Because of family resistance to donating relatives' organs there is a problem in converting potential donors into actual donors (Spital 1995). Presumed consent systems may help alleviate this. We know that the number of families rejecting requests for donations from their deceased relatives is lower in presumed consent countries than in informed consent countries (Abadie and Gay 2006; Thaler and Sunstein 2008). The third argument put forward by the advocates of presumed consent is that survey evidence consistently finds that the vast majority of citizens in Western democracies are pro-donation, with figures of between 65 per cent and 90 per cent found in different surveys (Gallup Organization 1993; New, Solomon, Dingwall and McHale 1994). The proponents argue that the default position should reflect the majority view. Lastly, supporters of opt-out systems have noted that opt-in systems do not provide a formal mechanism for those who wish to formally register an objection (British Medical Association 2008).

We can sum up: in informed consent countries there appears to be a gap between people's stated preferences and their actual behaviour, suggesting that failure to donate may be a simple reflection of inertia. A change of system in informed consent countries could help overcome the problems created by inertia and might better reflect the largely pro-donation views held by the general public – whilst also allowing those who wish to register an objection to do so more evidently.

So what is the level of support for a change of system? UK-based surveys report varying levels of support for presumed consent ranging from 30 per cent to over 60 per cent (Department of Health 2008). However, opinion polls do report a general shift in public opinion towards a preference for a presumed consent system (British Medical Association 2008). Members of Parliament are in favour of a change (National Kidney Research Fund, see British Medical Association 2008), and the British Medical Association, the professional body representing the majority of doctors in the UK, has for ten years advocated a system of what may be called 'soft presumed consent' (British Medical Association 2008), where people are presumed to be willing donors but where family preferences of the deceased are also taken into account. Yet the argument has not been won and many countries persist with a system of informed consent. This may reflect historical traditions and cultural preferences or could simply be an example of what public policy academics refer to as path dependency. This is a general propensity for policy-makers to continue along a path determined by existing policies that have become institutionalized through legal and administrative structures, practices and norms. This continues until a certain set of special conditions emerges to spark change (Baumgartner and Jones 1993; Kingdon 1995). Behavioural economists might explain such policy inertia more straightforwardly as a simple case of status quo bias on the part of policy decision-makers.

However, there are valid arguments against a change of choice architecture. Potential difficulties in introducing presumed consent legislation include the risk of eroding public trust in health professionals and undermining the principle of organ donation as a gift, and there are legal difficulties too (Department of Health 2008). Possible legal problems include challenges under the European Convention on Human Rights from families not consulted on the wishes of their deceased relatives. There are also concerns that imposing a new system of presumed consent without first attaining widespread public support could have a negative effect on organ procurement efforts and dampen general public support for the organ donation process (Fabre 1998; Abadie and Gay 2006).

From an ethical perspective we might ask whether it is right to shift the choice architecture to make assumptions about people's preferences over an issue of such considerable importance. Organ donation is arguably a personal matter, something which relates to one's very bodily integrity and sense of self. This is a hotly debated issue which has provoked much discussion in medical and ethics journals (Spital 1996; Fabre 1998) and medical ethics committees (British Medical Association 2008).

In a mandated choice system of registration, no prior assumption would be made about people's preferences, although citizens would be required to state whether or not they would like to become donors. The system has advocates in some informed consent countries such as the United States and the United Kingdom, where the American Medical Association and Britain's Royal College of Physicians respectively have called for trials and studies of the approach. Proponents of mandated choice suggest that the system could represent a more politically acceptable alternative to presumed consent systems while yielding similar registration levels to these systems (Thaler and Sunstein 2008; Johnson and Goldstein 2003). Others also suggest that since such a system would force individuals to make a decision, families would not be left with the difficult task of second-guessing a relative's wishes (Spital 1995), something which often leads them to refuse consent.

A further argument for forcing people to decide is the private and public discussion and deliberation that would be sparked. The argument is that if institutional spaces are created for people to discuss issues with one another, they may transform their views in a process of learning and deliberation, developing behaviours that are broadly civic in nature. As we saw in Chapter One, deliberation theorists believe that certain values only come to light in a process of deliberation, critical reflection and considered judgement. Once these values are allowed to surface, people can – and often do – transform their behaviour in line with these. Groups can create a consensus and the effect of the group itself may exert social pressure on the individuals within it. The public element of the debate, some deliberation theorists argue, should lead citizens to place greater weight on the public good than on individual self-interest (Miller 1992).

In terms of public acceptability, evidence from the United Kingdom and the United States reveals some support for mandated choice amongst the general public. In a series of deliberation events involving 350 people broadly representative of the UK population, participants ranked mandated choice as amongst their most favoured registration systems (Department of Health 2008). In a Gallup survey of a representative sample of 1,002 adults in the United States, 63 per cent of people stated that they would sign the organ donor register under a mandated choice system (Spital 1995).

The debate over organ donor registration systems is alive and well, but there is very little experimental evidence on which system might work best in terms of generating more registrations. We next present the results from two experimental interventions which help reveal something about how people might respond to different default positions, and different forms of persuasion. We are interested in how many people will sign an organ donor register when they are asked in different ways.

## Investigating behavioural change

To date, the majority of experiments which have related to organ donation preferences have asked people to state their hypothetical willingness or intention to become organ donors (Johnson and Goldstein 2003; Reubsaet, Brug, Nijkamp, Candel, Hooff and Borne 2005; Vinokur, Merion, Couper, Jones and Dong 2006). Our experiment took a different approach and was instead concerned with the behavioural outcome of organ donor registration. Our aim was to investigate behavioural rather than attitudinal change or mere hypothetical willingness to change.

As we have seen, evidence from observational studies indicates that organ donation registration rates are related to the type of organ donor registration system in operation, with presumed consent countries exhibiting higher levels of registration than informed consent systems. However, as the authors of previous studies concede, confounding factors may explain part of the story. It is possible that countries with presumed consent systems also have a strong cultural preference for organ donation to begin with (Abadie and Gay 2006). Similarly, a combination of factors may play a role in addition to legislation, including the availability of donors, transplantation system organization and infrastructure, health expenditure, wealth and public attitudes to organ transplantation (Rithalia *et al.* 2009). Observational data therefore has its limitations. As we discussed in Chapter 2, without experimental manipulation it is impossible to make causal inferences about the relationships between variables.

The 4,000 participants in our experiment were drawn from an Ipsos MORI panel and were broadly representative of the British population on key demographic variables. They were randomly allocated to one of three treatment groups: an informed consent group (effectively a control group since this represents the current system in Britain); a presumed consent group; and a mandated choice group. Presumed consent and mandated choice represent two different types of nudge. In the presumed consent group, the nudge is to change the default so that people are automatically signed up unless they opt out, while in the mandated choice group people are nudged to register by actively asking them to make a choice. Respondents in each group received an online survey on attitudes towards organ donation. The surveys were identical apart from the phrasing of the final question which asked respondents whether they would like to visit the national organ donation website to join the organ donor register. Each treatment group received a different form of words for the final survey question, reflecting one of the three registration systems or default positions in which we were interested, as shown in Table 8.1. Participants who opted to join the organ register were taken directly to the National Organ Donor Register website where they could register by completing a form. Registration rates for the three groups were tracked by the researchers in collaboration with NHS Blood and Transplant, the national organ donor registration body.

The findings provide the strongest backing for a presumed consent system where the default is that everyone is a donor, closely followed by a mandated choice system. Of the informed consent group which served as our control group, 15 per cent (196 of 1334) clicked through from the survey to visit the National Organ Donor Register website. This increased to 20 per cent (265 of 1335) when mandated choice was introduced (an increase of 5 percentage points) and to 23 per cent (300 of 1336) when presumed consent was introduced (an increase of 8 percentage points). Statistical tests indicate that there is an association between the treatment group and the number of people who clicked on the website and that this is statistically significant.

**Table 8.1** Organ donation registration survey choices

| |
|---|
| **Informed consent group (default = no one a donor)/Control Group:**<br>'Please take me to the NHS Organ Donation Website to join the National Organ Donor Register □ (check the box if you want to visit the site to register your name)' |
| **Presumed consent group (default = everyone a donor)/Nudge 1:**<br>'Please take me to the NHS Organ Donation Website to join the National Organ Donor Register ☑ (uncheck the box if you DO NOT want to visit the site to register your name)' |
| **Mandated choice group (no default position)/Nudge 2:**<br>'Please take me to the NHS Organ Donation Website to join the National Organ Donor Register (please answer either 'yes' or 'no')<br>Yes □     No □' |

## What did we find?

However, on the key behavioural outcome measure of interest, the result was much less clear. When we measured the number of people actually registering on the National Organ Donor Register website, less than 1 per cent of the total sample did so, with 0.52 per cent (seven respondents) from the presumed consent group, 0.67 per cent (nine respondents) from the mandated choice group and 0.3 per cent (four respondents) from the informed consent group signing up. So while mandated choice resulted in the greatest number of actual registrations, the registration rate across all three groups was negligible.

## What is the lesson?

Based on the number of respondents clicking through to the organ donor website, the first stage of the experiment indicates that employing a default position whereby people are presumed to be donors is likely to generate the largest number of registered organ donors. This is closely followed by a no default position, where people have to make a choice. However, the extra step of having to complete on organ donor registration form online after the first stage of the experiment was enough to deter people from joining. This indicates that any system of registration needs to minimize the effort required on the part of the public. In many informed consent countries it is common practice to provide the opportunity for people to sign the organ register when they are completing registrations for other purposes – driving licences, identity cards and so on. In the majority of cases a simple tick box (opt-in) question is incorporated into these. We suggest that replacing an opt-in with an opt-out or mandated choice version could generate a significant increase in organ donor registrations.

As we noted in Chapter 1, behavioural economists and nudgers attempt to devise strategies for behaviour change that go with the grain of human nature and our cognitive architecture, taking account of the biases, hunches and heuristics that influence our choices. Changing the default is a way of altering choice architecture that responds to our cognitive architecture (Thaler and Sunstein 2008). By presenting certain options as the default, governments can steer people towards a socially desired choice. If individuals view the default option as reflecting policy-makers' preferences or those of society at large, this may provide them with the rule of thumb they need to help make their decision.

This experiment shows that nudging by changing the default position can work. We found significant differences in website clicks between those who were nudged and those who were not. Those who were presented with a mandated choice or an opt-out question were significantly more likely to say yes to visiting the organ donor website than those presented with the opt-in question. The legal and ethical restrictions on the experiment meant that we had to offer one further step of completing a full online organ donor registration form. While few of those clicks (from any of our treatment groups) were converted into actual organ donor registrations, the website finding is of interest in itself. While it is only a speculation, it seems plausible that the results would have been similar had the website click itself represented an actual registration.

The implication is that building a choice architecture nudge on organ donation into registration forms such as passports and driving licences should help to increase organ donations in countries which are currently using opt-in systems. The key is to make it as easy as possible for people to register, so signing them up while they are filling in the paperwork for something else should work. While many opt-in countries already provide this opportunity, simply changing the default position and the question wording might increase registration levels significantly.

## Investigating nudge and think together

Our second experiment was constructed in order to test out nudging and thinking in one intervention. The experiment sought to investigate whether a nudge in the form of an information booklet could generate increases in organ donor registrations, as compared to a booklet combined with a discussion. We considered pitting the two against one another in an all-out battle, but after much discussion felt that a think on its own seemed less likely as a viable policy intervention than a combined nudge and a think. As we have noted elsewhere, deliberation requires people to absorb information before considering it. In practice, many deliberative events aiming to increase citizen participation involve presenting people with information and a series of options, and asking them to select from among these (see Smith 2009 for a review of deliberative institutions and innovations). Our hypothesis was that the information nudge would increase organ donor registration levels as compared to the control group, but that nudge and think combined would increase registration levels further still.

We recruited 179 higher education students in a UK university to take part in the experiment and they were randomly assigned to receive one of three treatments:

1. a four-page information booklet using techniques from behavioural economics to encourage registration;
2. the information booklet followed by a 15-minute group discussion on topical organ donation issues;
3. an information booklet about swine flu (placebo control).

The information nudge consisted of a four-page tailored information booklet using persuasion techniques based on behavioural economics principles (see Figure 8.1 for an excerpt from the booklet). In line with social influence theory, we included photographs and quotations from other students in support of organ donation. To generate a sense of peer support for the idea, the booklet highlighted that young people are one of the largest groups of people signing up to the organ donor register. It also stressed that over 90 per cent of the public are supportive of the principle of organ donation and that the number of donors is increasing daily. This was to create the sense of a social norm supportive of organ donation and to encourage participants to follow the trend. Official branding of the booklet by the UK's official organ donation body, NHS Blood and Transplant, enabled us to create the sense that the information it contained was from a credible and trustworthy source. The booklet contained the logo and website address of this body.

Celebrity endorsement with photographs and quotations was also used, drawing on information from the national organ donation website, with the selection of celebrities chosen as those most likely to appeal to a relatively young student population. In line with prospect theory, which allows us to see decisions in terms of choices between uncertain outcomes (see Chapter 1), the booklet also stressed the number of lives lost in recent years because of people waiting for organ transplants, thus emphasizing losses rather than possible life years gained through transplantation. In order to create an information disclosure effect the booklet signalled the opportunity for people to use social networking sites and twitter to tell their friends about their decision to join the organ donor register. The booklet flagged up a real website, created by the NHS as part of its publicity campaign, which enables people to upload a personal photograph to join a Wall of Life containing photographs of registered donors. People could subsequently add a widget to their own personal social networking space (for example, Facebook, Bebo and MySpace) that links to their photograph on the Wall of Life.

**Figure 8.1**   The information nudge for organ donation registration

From a purely scientific perspective one might have wanted to isolate the effect of each of these techniques and study them separately. However, putting individual theories from behavioural economics to the test was not our purpose; rather, we wanted to design a replicable and robust intervention that could be used by policy-makers to persuade people to sign the organ donor register. We hypothesized that a nudge combining several persuasion techniques based around some of the foremost theories developed from a behavioural economics perspective could produce a reasonably strong effect on organ donor registrations.

For the think treatment, a deliberation forum was created which involved research participants taking part in small structured group discussions lasting 15 minutes. Groups consisted of three to five people and three short case studies were provided in written format for groups to consider. Each case study highlighted a topical issue related to organ donation. The issues included decision-making about organ donation by the families of deceased people, whether or not everyone should be entitled to receive an organ transplant and the merits of different organ donor registration systems. Group discussion was led entirely by the groups themselves without the intervention of a facilitator, although researchers were present in the room to ensure that the discussions took place for the correct time period. The aim was to foster debate about controversies relating to the organ donation, to generate discussion about the merits of different types of systems and to permit critical reflection of the issues.

The control group received an information booklet of similar length to the treatment groups but the topic was an official NHS booklet on the prevention of swine flu. The aim was to generate comparable levels of information processing to the treatment groups and to have a means of checking whether any effect was down to the actual treatments themselves rather than simply being part of a group.

After receiving their treatment, all participants completed an attitudinal questionnaire and were provided with the opportunity to join the organ donor register using an official registration leaflet. The opportunity was presented in a neutral way and it was stressed that registration was entirely a matter of individual choice. Ballot boxes were provided at various points in the lecture theatres, in which participants could post their completed anonymous questionnaires along with any completed registration forms. Alternatively participants who chose to register could post their own registration forms directly to NHS Blood and Transplant. With the cooperation of NHS Blood and Transplant we tracked the number of students in each group signing up to the organ donor register, following up two months after the end of the experiment thus allowing sufficient time for late postal registrations. At the end of the experiment participants were told how they could de-register if they decided at a later date that they did not wish to be registered.

## What did we find?

The results were somewhat contrary to expectations in that we found the information nudge to have a greater effect than the combination of an information nudge and a discussion. Our initial hypothesis was that discussion amongst citizens combined with an information nudge would have a greater impact on organ donor registration than the information nudge alone. We anticipated that the effect of discussion would be to foster commitment to the principle of organ donation.

As outlined in Table 8.2, compared to our control group, participants in the nudge group increased registration by a margin of 4 percentage points. Although we did see increases in organ donation amongst the nudge and think group, when taking account of the control group, registrations in the nudge and think group decreased by a margin of 15 percentage points. There is a statistically significant association between treatment group and post-treatment registration rate.

**Table 8.2**  Pre and post organ donor registration by group

| Treatment group | Registered pre-intervention | | Registered post-intervention | | Total Number in group | Pre-post % change |
|---|---|---|---|---|---|---|
| | % | No. | % | No. | No. | % |
| Control | 34 | 20 | 64 | 38 | 59 | +30 |
| Nudge | 23 | 14 | 57 | 35 | 62 | +34 |
| Nudge + Think | 26 | 15 | 41 | 24 | 58 | +15 |

The attitudinal data collected after exposure to the treatments is summarized in Table 8.3. On three attitudinal questions – willingness to donate posthumously, favourable attitudes towards organ donation and intention to register – the nudge group displayed more pro-donation attitudes than both the control group and the nudge and think group, although the association between treatment group and favourable attitudes was not statistically significant on any of the measures. On two of the three measures the nudge and think group outperformed the control group, although once again these results were not statistically significant.

**Table 8.3**  Attitudes to organ donation

| | Willingness to donate posthumously | | Favourable attitude towards organ donation | | Intention to register (if not already registered) | |
|---|---|---|---|---|---|---|
| | % | No. | % | No. | % | No. |
| Control | 73% | 43 | 86% | 51 | 26% | 15 |
| Nudge | 77% | 48 | 94% | 58 | 57% | 35 |
| Nudge + Think | 67% | 39 | 88% | 51 | 47% | 27 |

## What is the lesson?

The second experimental intervention suggests that nudging by itself is more effective than nudging and thinking in encouraging organ donor registration. Tailored information booklets, based around behavioural economics principles, created increases in organ donor registrations and were more effective than combined information and discussion. It seems that the added effect of discussion generates some uncertainty. We can speculate about the possible reasons underlying the result. Since the discussions themselves allowed participants to explore the complexity of the topic and reflect in more detail, this enabled them to see different sides of the issue. The discussion topics purposefully raised topical issues that participants in the other two groups are unlikely to have considered. This seems to have provoked more mixed reactions amongst participants and a debriefing session with the research assistants who facilitated the discussion groups backs this up. For instance, groups raised controversial aspects of organ donation such as providing liver transplants to alcoholics, which may have created some negative views.

Overall, the findings indicate that an information nudge based around behavioural economics principles seems to make a difference in changing behaviour in a controversial and sensitive area of civic behaviour. By contrast, we find that when citizens engage in relatively unfacilitated discussions about the issue, their response is quite different and behaviour is harder to shift. Our findings illustrate the dilemma facing policy-makers seeking to encourage behaviour change: should they really be nudging citizens in areas such as these that have profound implications for individual liberty? Perhaps these areas are worthy of more sustained discussion and reflection.

Behavioural economists would argue that people often fail to make active choices on these issues largely because of inertia and procrastination, suggesting that citizens just do not take the time to think the issues through. The implication of these arguments could be that a paternalistic state should help citizens make choices by providing them with a steer to guide them in the right direction. However, our research suggests that individual preferences, when allowed more space to develop following a period of even brief deliberation, may actually be at odds with the policy-makers' priorities. A potential implication of this is that to help citizens feel comfortable with their choices, there should be considerable time allowed for deliberation, education or discussion alongside nudging. As Saward reminds us, allowing citizens to reflect on their preferences before making choices is part of a process of improving the democratic legitimacy of the political systems of which they are a part (Saward 2001). Perhaps there is an argument here for allowing citizens the opportunity to help design the nudges in order to increase the legitimacy of any changes to choice architecture. In the case of organ donation, a national debate or even a referendum on changing the registration system from an opt-in to an opt-out or a mandated choice system might be a useful way forward. This might serve to alleviate the concerns of those who are opposed to the use of nudges in this context.

A final point worth noting to end the chapter is that registration outcomes were significantly higher overall for the second experiment than for our first online organ donor registration experiment, suggesting that interventions delivered in person may hold greater promise than online interventions. In view of the relative costs of the two studies (with the first, the online survey, costing approximately four times as much as the face-to-face study), interventions delivered in person may prove a more cost-effective way of generating organ donor registrations.

*Further reading*

The best overview of the evidence on presumed consent is Rithalia, A., McDaid, C., Suekarran, S., Norman, G., Myers, L. and Sowden, A. (2009), 'A Systematic Review of Presumed Consent Systems for Deceased Organ Donation', *Health Technology Assessment*, 13 (26), DOI: 10.3310/hta1326. For an empirical analysis of the influence of different legislative defaults on donation rates see Abadie, A. and Gay, S. (2006), 'The Impact of Presumed Consent Legislation on Cadeveric Organ Donation: A Cross-Country Study', *Journal of Health Economics*, 25: 599–620. For more detail on the mandated choice option, see Spital, A. (1996), 'Mandated Choice for Organ Donation:

Time to Give It a Try', *Annals of Internal Medicine*, 125: 66–9. An example of an educational intervention aiming to increase organ donation is discussed in Quinn, M.T., Alexander, G.C., Hollingsworth, D., O'Connor, K.G. and Meltzer, D. (2006), 'Design and Evaluation of a Workplace Intervention to Promote Organ Donation', *Progress in Transplantation*, 16: 253–9.

# 9

# Debating

## Why study deliberation and online debating?

In defining think in Chapter 1, we highlighted the claim within theoretical work on deliberative democracy that it provides the conditions under which contentious moral and political issues can be dealt with effectively. In a deliberative setting, citizens take each others' perspectives seriously, reflect on their own prejudices and try to avoid unnecessary conflict (Gutmann and Thompson 1996). This is all well and good in theory, but does it translate into practice? Public authorities are showing increasing interest in promoting deliberation amongst citizens with democratic innovations such as participatory budgeting, citizens' juries, deliberative polling and other such initiatives spreading across the world (Fung 2003b; Smith 2009). The provision of opportunities for citizens to deliberate about matters of public concern is perceived by policy-makers and reformers as a potential response to widespread disillusionment and disenchantment with the political process.

Whether or not particular examples of innovation have had a meaningful effect on the political process, it is undeniable that a number of public authorities are being more creative in their attempts to engage citizens. And with the proliferation of information and communication technology, public authorities are increasingly looking to harness the internet to develop new ways of promoting deliberation amongst citizens. Internet engagement is particularly attractive to authorities because it has the potential to engage large numbers of citizens without the costs (financial and psychological) of bringing them together in the same physical space. There is the possibility of scaling up participation – and, for policy-makers in particular, numbers count when it comes to judging the legitimacy of engagement strategies.

But what happens when deliberation on controversial public policy issues goes online? Does the claim of deliberative democratic theorists that public deliberation is particularly effective for dealing with morally contentious issues hold in this new environment? Our experiment responds to the lacuna in social science research (in particular, experimental research) on the use of internet technologies for engaging citizens in the political process. The experiment focuses on arguably the most common form of online engagement: asynchronous discussion forums. The aim of the experiment was twofold. First, to understand the extent to which giving citizens the opportunity to debate controversial policy issues (in this case youth anti-social behaviour and community cohesion) led to changes in policy knowledge and preferences. And second, to analyse the extent to which citizens actually deliberate online and whether their interactions are inclusive and informed.

## What do we know about online engagement?

Given that commentators are often quick to claim that the internet is either the saviour or the enemy of democracy, it is surprising that there is relatively little rigorous social scientific research on online citizen engagement with public authorities (rare examples include Price 2006; Neblo, Esterling, Kennedy, Lazer and Sokhey 2010). The more general literature on politics and the internet highlights a number of issues that present challenges to designing online participation and deliberation. The first is the emergence of a digital divide: not everyone has access to the internet and, once online, not everyone has the same level of proficiency in the use of new technologies. There is a concern that existing political inequalities are reinforced online, or new inequalities are created (Norris 2001; Barber 1998; Cederman and Kraus 2005). Second, even when online, most people do not suddenly become interested in politics. In other words, those people who engage in political discussions online are those who already have a high degree of political interest (EOS Gallop Europe 2002). Third, there is a concern that in the online world, people tend to be attracted to discussions that simply reinforce their already established viewpoints and prejudices: they find like-minded people and avoid those with different perspectives (Sunstein 2001; Dahlberg 2007). Fourth, when people with different views do come together, they do not often deliberate: rather they try to dominate the discussion (Coleman 2004; Sack 2005) or resort to flaming – offensive contributions towards those with different views (Docter and Dutton 1998). The preponderance of flaming, in particular, offers a significant challenge to the idea that the internet can host inclusive and reasoned deliberation on morally contentious issues.

These are important insights, but they tend to be rather generic in nature: claims about internet engagement per se, rather than specific designs for engaging citizens. Recent work on internet-based forums suggests that design is crucial: generalizations about online behaviour often fail to recognize the particular characteristics of different online environments (Wright and Street 2007: 850). As Coleman argues:

The environment and structure of communication has a significant effect upon its content; synchronous chat rooms and peer-generated Usenet groups are no more indicative of the scope for online public deliberation than loud, prejudiced and banal political arguments in crowded pubs are indicative of the breadth of offline political discussion. (Coleman 2004: 6)

So, for example, Janssen and Kies have argued that whether the online discussion space is real-time (chat-rooms) or asynchronous (email lists; newsgroups; bulletin boards; forums) has a substantial effect on the way that citizens interact. They argue:

It is generally recognized that the former are spaces of encounter that attract small talk and jokes, while the latter constitutes a more favourable place for the appearance of some form of rational-critical form of debate since it allows participants to spend more time to think and justify their interventions. (Janssen and Kies 2005: 321)

Other characteristics such as anonymity, extent of freedom of speech and form of moderation are likely to have an effect on the quality of engagement and deliberation. Institutional design is likely to have a profound effect on the capacity of citizens to deliberate on morally and politically contentious subjects.

Taking an experimental approach to analysing online engagement means bringing together a random selection of citizens. This then directly connects our experiment to the developing practice of mini-publics: democratic innovations based on forms of random selection. The desire to ensure deliberations are inclusive has influenced the design of (for example) citizens' juries, consensus conferences, deliberative polls and, recently, the highly impressive citizens' assemblies that were established in British Columbia and then Ontario to deliberate on new electoral systems (Warren and Pearse 2008; Fishkin 2009; Smith 2009). Research on such mini-publics suggests that citizens take the opportunity to participate seriously and frequently change their preferences in light of the provision of information and opportunities to deliberate. And there is evidence that mini-publics can deal with highly contentious issues. Consensus conferences (most prevalent in Denmark) have deliberated on new and often controversial scientific and technological developments that raise serious social and ethical concerns, for example, the use of transgenic animals in biotechnology research (Joss and Durant 1995). Deliberative polls have been run successfully in divided societies: on Australian aboriginal issues; housing, crime and education policy towards the Roma in Bulgaria; and educational policy in Northern Ireland (Fishkin 2009: 161–6).

Aside from a couple of experiments where Fishkin and his colleagues have attempted to transfer the deliberative poll model online (Fishkin 2009: 169–75), there has been no significant experimentation with online mini-publics, particularly in relation to controversial policy issues. The results from online deliberative polling (ODP) indicate that the policy knowledge and preferences of participants tend to move in the same direction as for participants in offline equivalents, but that 'changes from online deliberation were less pronounced than in the face-to-face version' (Ackerman and Fishkin 2004: 117; for more detail, see Luskin, Fishkin and Iyengar 2006: 17–23). However, the design of the ODP exploits real-time (synchronous) technology that is unlikely to be used in practice by many public authorities due to its high cost and the requirement of specialist software and hardware. More likely, if public authorities are to make widespread use of online mini-publics they will utilize low-cost asynchronous discussion platforms with which they are already familiar. It is such a platform on which our experiment is based.

## What is the intervention?

In early 2009, 6,009 members of the Ipsos MORI online panel accepted an invitation to participate in the experiment. They were invited to complete three questionnaires over a three-week period and were told that they may be asked to engage in other online tasks during that period. On completion of the three questionnaires, participants were entered into a prize draw. The cohort of citizens was selected from Ipsos MORI's panel using quotas for gender, age and geographical location. Given the nature of the panel, we had to accept that the sample was more educated than the general population and that by definition they had access to the internet. We were pleased, however, that there was a good spread of levels of internet usage (from occasional to heavy users) and that the sample was representative of the population in terms of political interest.

The 6,009 participants completed a first questionnaire and were then randomly allocated to six experimental groups. Two groups of 1,002 were invited to participate in two discussion forums. The first group started with discussions on youth anti-social behaviour; the second on community cohesion. After ten days of discussion, participants completed a second questionnaire and then swapped topics. After another ten days of discussion, participants completed a third questionnaire and were thanked for their commitment and contributions.

In designing the discussion forums, hosted on specially commissioned boards (using the phpBB 3.0x internet forum package), we included a number of features in an attempt to promote informed and respectful contributions and deliberation between participants. For example:

1. Participation was incentivized with entries into the prize draw each time participants spent ten minutes or more online.
2. New topics for discussion were added every two days and participants were sent a reminder email each time a new topic was added.
3. Participants could log-on and contribute whenever they wished.
4. When logging on for the first time, participants were greeted with a video from the then Secretary of State for Communities and Local Government, Hazel Blears, who gave her support for the project and committed herself to consider the issues raised by participants.
5. Participants were directed to the rules of discussion that stressed the importance of mutual respect to other participants.
6. Participants did not need to give background information on their gender, age, ethnicity, etc. to other participants.
7. Easily accessible background information was in what we called a 'fuel for thought' box on each page: short briefing documents and audio-visual materials, including specially commissioned videos of community representatives offering different viewpoints.
8. Visible (although relatively light) moderation prompted contributions, particularly from those who had not posted, and summarized the arguments to date.
9. Participants were able to easily report any posts that they believed offensive or to have broken the rules of discussion.

While we had advice from some quarters to use a pre-moderation strategy – that is to vet every contribution before it appeared on the site – to ensure there was no flaming, we decided against this strategy on two grounds. First, on purely pragmatic grounds we were attempting to design a process that could be easily adopted by public authorities. Pre-moderation increases costs substantially. Second, we wished to see if the combination of the other design features we had employed would encourage more civically minded behaviour on the part of participants without recourse to pre-moderation, even on highly contentious issues of public policy.

A further 2,002 participants were allocated to the two control groups: these participants only completed the three questionnaires; they had no access to the online discussion forums. This aspect of the design of the experiment is essential for the inference we wish to make: that the opportunity to debate – and its practice – has effects on attitudes and knowledge.

In itself, this would represent an interesting experiment: by comparing the discussion and control groups, we are in the position to understand whether the opportunity to learn about and discuss pressing political issues online leads to changes in knowledge and policy preferences, and to observe the extent to which interactions reached the standards of informed and reasoned deliberation. But we added a twist to our experimental design. The final 2,003 participants were allocated to two information-only groups. They were treated in exactly the same way as the discussion groups with one significant exception. The boards had the same features with participants able to post comments. The difference was that they were not able to see the postings of other participants. Why did we do this? In order to investigate the added value of engaging with other participants, how important is providing the opportunity to discuss an issue compared with only receiving information for personal reflection? After all, if there is no difference, public authorities might only need to provide information and opportunities for response rather than creating more expensive discussion forums.

## What did we find?

The experiment generated three significant sets of findings for those interested in think strategies: first, who participates in online forums; second, whether there are any changes in policy knowledge and preferences; and, third, the extent to which interactions can be classified as deliberative.

### Who participates in online forums?

Not everyone who was invited to participate in the discussion groups took up that invitation. And not everyone who logged on to the site posted. Out of the 2,004 participants assigned to the discussion group, roughly half (1,073) logged on to the discussion board at least once during the study period, with 526 (26 per cent) contributing one or more posts. This means that around half of those who logged on did not contribute to discussions: in the online world such spectators are referred to as lurkers (Jansen and Kies 2005: 331). Having half the participants logging on and half of those posting may appear disappointing: however, given the low levels of political participation across society this could equally be seen as an impressive percentage.

Unlike offline mini-publics, where those who accept an invitation are then directly involved in interactions (they cannot escape without getting up and leaving the room!), the structure of the online world means that there is self-selection in both logging on to the discussion forum and then choosing whether or not to make a contribution. This element of self-selection may undermine the random selection, reinforcing existing differentials of participation (see, for example, Verba, Nie and Kim 1978). To some degree this is what happened in the experiment. An analysis of those who participated indicates that those who chose to log-on or post tended to be older and politically interested. The picture for education is more ambiguous: those who logged on tended to have higher qualifications, but this is not the case for those who posted. For the classic explanatory factors of age, political interest and, to a lesser degree, education, the traditional participation bias is felt: the online world mirrors offline differentials. But there are two important caveats that complicate the picture somewhat.

The first is in relation to gender: women were more likely to make contributions. We can speculate on why this might be the case: the asynchronous form of engagement allows women to engage in their own time rather than the inconvenient times of many public meetings; anonymity may remove barriers; the topics (social policy issues relating to youth and community cohesion) may appeal more to a female audience. Second, and surprisingly, frequency of internet use is not a significant factor. We had expected those participants with more familiarity with the online world to participate more: this was not the case.

## Any change in knowledge and preferences?

In deliberative polls, Fishkin and his colleagues find fairly significant changes in policy knowledge and preferences following a period of deliberation (Fishkin 2009). Taken as a whole sample (all 6,009 participants), we find no systematic differences between control, information-only and discussion groups. There would appear to be no added value of either providing information or opportunities to deliberate online. But this overall finding may hide differences between the significant numbers who decided not to participate, those who logged on to the site and those who posted. More intense participation may result in differences in policy knowledge and preferences.

By comparing the whole sample with those citizens who logged-on and those who posted we can detect some, albeit modest, differences. Our analysis to date has primarily been on the youth anti-social behaviour boards. Focusing on those participants who logged on, we find no differences in knowledge or preferences when we compare results with the equivalent element of the control group. This is the case for participants in both information-only and discussion groups. However, when we focus only on those who posted on the discussion boards, then we find some modest but consistent differences in relation to policy preferences (but nothing of the order that Fishkin claims for deliberative polls).

**Figure 9.1** Change in preferences by policy question

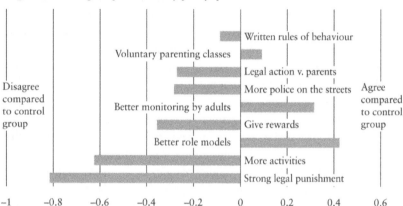

Disagree compared to control group

Agree compared to control group

Written rules of behaviour
Voluntary parenting classes
Legal action v. parents
More police on the streets
Better monitoring by adults
Give rewards
Better role models
More activities
Strong legal punishment

-1   -0.8   -0.6   -0.4   -0.2   0   0.2   0.4   0.6

▩ Preferences of discussion board participants compared to preference of the control group

As we see in Figure 9.1, the policy preferences of those who posted tend to move away from legal punishment and heavier policing and towards the promotion of better role models and improved monitoring of young people by adults. While there is support for such community-based intervention (over legal and policing solutions), participants are less supportive of the provision of activities or rewards for young people. These weak preference shifts only occurred amongst the participants in the discussion boards, not for those in the information-only groups. But when it comes to policy knowledge, there are again no differences between the two groups. What this indicates is that participation in an online discussion forum can have a modest effect on policy preferences for those who contribute. And that it is interaction in the discussion forums, rather than increases in knowledge, that drives these modest changes. But should this interaction be understood as deliberative?

## *How deliberative?*

The analysis to date offers some indications that the discussion forum might be less than deliberative as understood within theories of deliberative democracy (see Chapter 1). First, we have seen that the discussions that took place online are not fully inclusive in that there is a significant amount of self-selection. This is not all in the direction of reinforcing traditional political inequalities (particularly in relation to gender), but certainly does not realize full inclusiveness. Second, while we are able to find some modest and consistent changes in policy preferences amongst those who contributed to the discussion forums, there were no changes in policy knowledge. In other words, one of the defining features of deliberation – that it is informed – is not present. Participants may know more about what other citizens think about the issues at hand, but the low level of use of background materials by those who posted contributions confirms our finding.

Observing the discussions that took place online gives further insight into the extent to which interactions might be classified as deliberative. On a positive note, the fears of those who believe that internet discussion forums by their nature will degenerate into flaming on controversial topics are not confirmed: the two topics – youth anti-social behaviour and in particular community cohesion – are controversial public issues and yet posts typically remained within the rules of discussion established for the forum. Even when contributions might be defined as disrespectful (generally towards those under discussion, not other participants), they were a long way from being overly offensive. There was no flaming and not one post was reported to the moderators for its content. In this sense an online think strategy can deal with contentious policy issues. But while interactions tended to be respectful, there was little evidence of reciprocity or reason-giving which are significant elements of think. On the threads that we have analysed, participants tended to contribute without recognition of the contributions of others and without offering reasons to back their claims. These findings suggest that the minimal conditions were in place for deliberation, such as mutual respect, but that in actual practice deliberation was not realized.

### What are the lessons?

The results of our experiment for those who wish to promote online deliberation on highly contentious issues are mixed. Most importantly they indicate that, if it is carefully designed, a large-scale online asynchronous mini-public can be successfully organized on controversial policy issues.

Attention to institutional design can encourage citizens to be mutually respectful, even on challenging topics. This indicates that one of our key findings from a think experiment may actually be about nudge: those who fear that the online world will always deteriorate into flaming need to recognize that pro-civic behaviour cues can be built into the design of discussion forums. The design characteristics of any forum arguably have a significant effect on whether mutual respect will be realized.

Whether we can realistically expect online deliberation to achieve the deliberative qualities of offline mini-publics is another matter. Here public authorities face a number of challenges. First, although a random selection of participants can be invited, those who post are self-selecting. And it is this self-selecting group who experience change (albeit modest) in preferences. Second, the evidence we have provided indicates that this weak preference change is not well-informed: participants tend to go straight to the discussion thread rather than spending time reading or watching policy-relevant background materials. Forcing participants to access information before contributing to discussion threads would no doubt have further reduced participation levels. The differences here between offline and online designs are stark. Offline, we can ensure that the group is representative of the wider population; participants cannot escape being exposed to information; and facilitators can more easily encourage the more reluctant to contribute to discussions. Online, it is simply more difficult to create the conditions for deliberation: participants can decide whether to post; there is little the moderator can do to ensure an equal voice for all participants; and it is easy to avoid background information. While participants may be learning from each other, the failure to increase their policy knowledge raises the legitimate question about the extent to which online deliberation is informed.

Our experiment offers insights into the way in which online discussion forums have very different characteristics from face-to-face forums. Engagement in asynchronous discussion forums tends to be less intense with participants choosing if and when to engage – and this has effects on the quality of interaction. We have shown that if designed carefully (with serious content, moderation, etc.), participants behave in a civil manner towards each other, even on controversial areas of social policy. However, the design did not encourage changes in policy preferences or increase in policy-relevant knowledge. This indicates the need for further experimental research that varies institutional design characteristics: is it possible to encourage more informed interactions under different sets of conditions? We should certainly not view this experiment as evidence that think does not work! After all, the forum allowed significant numbers of contributions on highly contentious topics with no recourse to flaming. That in itself shows the power of a carefully designed think strategy.

The next chapter describes a design experiment to bring the voices of the socially marginalized into the forum for making decisions.

*Further reading*

The online *Journal of Public Deliberation* (http://services.bepress.com/jpd) has a number of articles on online deliberation, with occasional experimental work. The work of Fishkin and his colleagues on online deliberative polling (and its original offline variant) can be found at the Center for Deliberative Democracy (http://cdd.stanford.edu). For organizations promoting think strategies, see in particular the US-based National Coalition for Dialogue and Deliberation (http://www.thataway.org) and the Deliberative Democracy Consortium (http://www.deliberative-democracy.net). *Participedia* (http://www.participedia.net) is a growing resource for information on democratic innovations. Finally, for a sustained critique of Amy Gutmann and Dennis Thompson's theory of deliberative democracy, see the essays in Macedo, S. (ed.) (1999), *Deliberative Politics: Essays on Democracy and Disagreement*, Oxford: Oxford University Press.

## 10

# Including

## Why study local inclusion?

Decentralization is a common political strategy for public authorities aiming to increase citizen engagement. In theory, bringing decision-making closer to the local population reduces the costs associated with political participation because people do not have to make so much effort to attend meetings and may perceive the public authority as closer to their views and interests. However, decentralization in itself rarely manages to engage the politically marginalized as it often simply reinforces extant political inequalities.

This chapter reports on a design experiment that aims to bring the voices of the politically marginalized into the local forums recently established by a large rural local authority in the UK. One of the first activities of the forums was to consider how the authority engages the local population: the challenge of the experiment was to consider how the voices of the excluded are heard in this process. The research team worked with the public authority to develop and implement a design experiment to test whether electronic media (in this case, a DVD) could be utilized to ensure that the voices of the politically marginalized where brought into these local deliberations.

## What do we know about inclusion?

Democracy rests on the principle of political equality. But studies of participation across a range of political activities provide comprehensive evidence that very few citizens actually engage regularly in political action – whether conventional or unconventional – and that participation is strongly positively correlated to income, wealth and education (Verba *et al.* 1978; Pattie *et al.* 2005). Democracy's unresolved dilemma remains unequal participation (Lijphart 1997). In both elections and consultation exercises, politically marginalized social groups systematically fail to engage. This can have a significant impact on the nature of decisions: if the politically excluded are not present and able to voice their perspectives, decisions are unlikely to fully respond to their concerns (Phillips 1995: 13). While advocates of citizen participation argue for increasing opportunities for citizens to engage, there is reasonable scepticism that this will simply reinforce and amplify the existing differentials of power and influence within society (Sartori 1987: 114; Phillips 1991: 162).

In Chapter 1 we highlighted the development of democratic innovations as part of the broader think strategy: institutions specifically designed to increase and deepen citizen participation in the political process (Smith 2009). There is emerging evidence that such innovations, when carefully designed, can successfully engage those people who are politically marginalized. In the previous chapter we focused on the design of mini-publics: (near) random selection is used to ensure that all socio-economic groups are present. But there is evidence that open meetings can also be designed that reverse differentials in participation. Arguably the most celebrated is participatory budgeting in Porto Alegre. The building block of the initiative is a series of budget assemblies in which 'socio-economic inequalities did not reproduce themselves ... Much to the contrary, the household incomes of budget participants are significantly lower than those of the population as a whole ... participants in the regional assemblies were poorer than the population as a whole' (Abers 2000: 122). People in poorer communities have much to gain and so participate in high numbers (Smith 2009: 43–4). This incentive to participate has not always been present as participatory budgeting has spread worldwide and, as such, existing differentials in participation have often been reproduced.

Chicago Community Policing offers another example of how careful institutional design can affect inclusion. In 1995, the Chicago Police Department began holding monthly community beat meetings in 285 neighbourhood beats across the city. In these beat meetings, police officers work with local residents to improve public safety in the neighbourhood. Evidence suggests that in comparison to traditional forms of consultation, Chicago Community Policing attracts a significant proportion of citizens from poor and less well-educated neighbourhoods who are able directly to influence local policing strategies (Fung 2003a; Fung 2006).

But these examples buck the trend. In both Porto Alegre and Chicago the municipal public authority has invested heavily in community outreach programmes and offered substantial opportunities to affect the delivery of local services. As Fung argues: 'disadvantaged citizens will overcome quite substantial barriers to participate in institutions that credibly promise to reward such activity with concrete improvements to the public goods upon which those citizens rely' (Fung 2003a: 115). Most public authorities are unwilling to invest the resources necessary to build the capacity of people in marginalized communities or to restructure decision-making processes so that the direct effect of participation is felt in more effective service delivery provision. Public authorities may have good intentions and wish to hear the voices of the politically marginalized, but the forums they create often fail to motivate engagement on the part of the citizens. Where public authorities develop more mundane decentralization strategies (as compared to the democratic innovations that Porto Alegre's participatory budgeting and Chicago's community policing represent), how can the voices of the politically marginalized be heard in local deliberations?

## What is the intervention?

Wiltshire Council was created by the UK government in 2009, replacing a series of smaller district authorities and the county council. In recognition of the significant geographical area of the council and the differences in needs of the local communities, the council established Area Boards. These boards are made up of the local councillors from Wiltshire Council, elected representatives from town and parish councils, representatives from other local public institutions such as the police and fire service, and other community representatives. The meetings are open to local people. The aim of the boards is to influence what Wiltshire Council does in the local area and to ensure that decisions about local issues are made locally (http://www.wiltshire.gov.uk/communityandliving/areaboards.htm).

Political leaders and officers at Wiltshire recognized the importance of hearing the voices of the politically marginalized in the process of establishing the working practices of the 18 Area Boards across Wiltshire. Members of our research team agreed to work with the Area Board Team to develop and implement a design experiment that evaluated a mechanism for including the voices of the politically marginalized in the Area Boards as they discussed the ways in which they would engage their local populations. The number of boards being established at the same time meant that a design experiment would be possible since an intervention could be varied across geographical areas.

Wiltshire Council was not willing to make resources available for significant mobilization efforts targeted at the politically disengaged. In this sense its decentralization strategy mirrors the approach taken by most public authorities: create local forums that are open to local citizens, but with no dedicated outreach strategy beyond the usual adverts and posters. In these circumstances, how do public authorities ensure that the voices of the politically marginalized are to be heard when we know that citizens from these social groups are unlikely to attend in person?

After much discussion and negotiation, the Area Board Team and the researchers decided to focus on facilitating the perspectives of 'those who do not normally engage in formal Council mechanisms'. Board managers were to facilitate Area Board discussions on how to engage more effectively the local community, drawing on a specifically commissioned DVD that presented a range of marginalized voices: from ethnic minority groups, young people, the military, people with disabilities and others who may not engage for reasons of disinterest, apathy or feelings of disempowerment. The idea behind a DVD is that it could be used in very different circumstances (not just the Area Boards) and it is a cost-effective initiative that could easily be replicated by other public authorities. The experimental intervention was to be a debate at the first meeting of selected Area Boards facilitated by the relevant board manager on the question of how the board could better engage the local community. This debate would be informed by the views and ideas articulated on the DVD, challenging those present to consider the perspectives of those not in the room. The council commissioned a professional filmmaker with experience in participatory video (Lunch and Lunch 2006) to undertake the interviews; the DVD was co-produced by the board managers and the research team. The final version of the DVD consists of different sections or chapters, each with a collection of community voices discussing aspects of engagement with the Council. This structure allowed board managers to facilitate discussions around specific aspects of participation: the structure, timing and location of meetings; and the responsiveness of the council to demands from the community.

**Table 10.1** Brief for community interviews

We are looking at how the new council for Wiltshire could engage more people more effectively in decisions which will have an effect on their lives and communities. This will be a new council that is working closely with other service providers such as Fire, the Police and Health so it really does cover lots of different aspects of local life – from community safety to roads, schools, health and emergency services. There are some really active communities in Wiltshire and we are interested in how local people and groups could be supported to work on the sort of projects and initiatives that would improve the quality of life in the area.

How are your views currently represented? Councillors are elected in each area to represent local people and the interests, priorities and issues for the community. There are town and parish councils in each area to represent these local interests. In some areas, community area partnerships have been established and also groups to represent various interests including user groups for people with disabilities, groups for older people and young people's issues groups. There are citizens' panels run by the council for residents, young people and carers. These are some of the local ways that the council has sought to engage with local people and ensure that all voices within a community can be heard.

But maybe the ways that people can participate and make their voices heard need to be improved? For example, what do you think about how you are able to engage with the council and the other service providers? Are you interested in participating? What puts you off? How could it be better? What would you like to have more of an influence over? These are some of the questions we want to look at. We will create a 20-minute film of your ideas and viewpoints which then can be shown to community groups and councillors and other interested parties to begin to challenge and develop new ways forward in engaging people.

The intervention was targeted at six Area Boards. Six further boards with reasonably similar geographical and socio-economic characteristics were selected as comparisons: in these boards, discussions about engaging the local community took place, but without the DVD (and thus the voices of the politically marginalized). Researchers attended the meetings, observing the progress of the deliberations and administering a short questionnaire to ascertain the views of attendees (councillors, officers, community representatives and citizens) on the impact of the DVD. The design experiment involved iteration, with the Area Board Team meeting with the researchers after two board meetings to decide if the intervention needed to be adjusted.

## What did we find?

The intervention had mixed results. One of the challenges of a design experiment is that it is not as decisive and discrete an intervention as a randomized controlled trial (see Chapter 2), which makes it harder to ascertain the effect of the intervention. In attempting to understand the impact of the DVD-enabled deliberation, we must try to separate out the effect of a series of unexpected practical problems.

First, board meetings were held in very different locations, some of which had poor acoustics and/or poor audio-visual equipment, making it difficult for some in attendance to hear the voices on the DVD. Second, the chairs of some boards (an elected representative) wanted other issues to be dealt with and this created long agendas and pressure on time for the discussion about community engagement. This led to a degree of frustration as the item was squeezed inappropriately. Third, some of the participants filmed for the DVD were arguably not as politically marginalized as the research team had expected. Whilst community managers had been given the brief to introduce the professional filmmaker to 'those who do not normally engage in formal Council mechanisms', in a number of cases these were community activists who were well known to some of the councillors. Additionally, in editing the DVD, the community managers tended to privilege the voices of those who could more clearly articulate problems with engagement. The voices of more experienced community activists tended to come to the fore: an example of production values trumping democratic inclusion? An elected member in an early Area Board took exception to one of the individuals on the DVD who he had had personal dealings with, forcing a re-edit which reduced the DVD's critical edge. But even with these practical problems that placed a challenge on the experimental conditions, the intervention generated some interesting findings.

First, the nature of the debate on community engagement in those boards that used the DVD was more extensive and considerate to the views of the politically marginalized than in those that did not. Even when the reaction from certain participants was hostile to the voices on the DVD, questions of inclusion and exclusion were explicitly raised and confronted. Where the DVD was not used, discussion of engagement was fairly superficial with little meaningful consideration of how the politically marginalized could be more effectively engaged.

Second, the majority of participants who completed the questionnaire in the Area Board meetings where the DVD was used tended to believe that it had helped their thinking on matters of inclusion and exclusion (see Figure 10.1). There were a number of written comments along the lines that the DVD 'opened people's eyes to what the general people in the community think; real issues described by real people'; that it was 'interesting to have vox pops from people who couldn't (wouldn't) attend a meeting in person' and that such an intervention 'acts as a starting point for debate; triggered public to talk'. The level of ambivalence ('neutral') towards the DVD appears to be related to those board meetings where there were problems with acoustics and/or the audio-visual equipment.

**Figure 10.1**  Satisfaction with the DVD (number of participants)

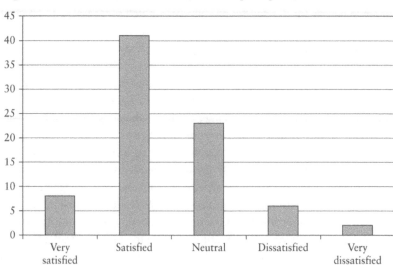

How satisfied as an aid to thinking?

Third, there is evidence in at least two area boards that the DVD influenced thinking about future public engagement. One board manager planned to take the DVD into other institutions that worked at the local level:

> I think what has come out of it or what will come out of it is that there is now a will for that DVD to be taken to the partnership and to the task group. And so a question which is quite broad and which we might have talked about a little bit here and there ... will now be taken on, have some more focus to it.

And, in a second area board, the DVD and the ensuing discussion led to an agreement between the local school and the board to find new ways of communicating with younger people. More widely, the DVD stimulated discussion throughout the council structures (even if in some quarters it was defensive). It certainly had an impact on the community managers themselves, one of whom stated at an iteration meeting:

> It's made me think about so many more ways to think about getting people into the meetings ... well not even into the meetings but can we get governance into the community, you know establishing governance networks in an area rather than focus on individual structures like committees. That's not what it's about – it's how we get information out to communities and how they're involved in different ways and coordinated.

Fourth, the critical nature of the voices on the DVD created resistance amongst elected representatives. While we have already discussed the problem that at least one of the people filmed on the DVD was known to one of the councillors by the phrase 'usual suspect', the negative and defensive reaction on the part of a number of councillors was certainly not all due to such personality clashes. Quite simply they were not happy about being put in an uncomfortable situation that they were not in a position to control. A number were reluctant to engage with the perspectives being voiced – on two occasions they were openly hostile. Rather than being a springboard to debate, they perceived the criticism from the politically marginalized as a direct personal attack. As one community manager asked: 'I just wonder how we're going to get those voices in if the reaction is councillors putting down their pens and folding their arms.' There appeared to be an immediate negative gut reaction on the part of some elected representatives. Such reactions are a long way from the facilitative leadership role that is being promoted for councillors in local government reform in the UK (Stoker and Greasley 2008) and indicates the extent to which those who hold a powerful position in local governance are often reluctant to loosen their grip on the political agenda.

Finally, this reaction by a number of elected members indicates the difficult position that Area Board managers are placed in. As the facilitators of this portion of the agenda, the quality of the debate rests on their skills and capacities. Creating the conditions under which all participants (in particular, elected representatives) are willing to be challenged is not an easy task – and not one that all the managers were up to. Some of this was due to time constraints and the prejudices of elected representatives present at the meeting; but in other cases it reflected just how difficult it is to enable inclusive deliberation. This has been recognized by the council, which is now providing training in facilitation both to its Area Board managers and also to local councillors during their period of induction.

## What are the lessons?

While we have witnessed the development of a number of exemplary democratic innovations that have reversed the traditional participation bias, these have required significant political and institutional commitment (Smith 2005; Smith 2009). Most public authorities do not show this level of commitment to engaging citizens in political decision-making processes, being less willing to invest the resources (financial, institutional and political) necessary to ensure participation by the traditionally politically marginalized. Thus, we witness, for example, decentralization strategies, where public authorities create local forums open to local citizens, but without developing the necessary outreach programmes and incentive structures that enable engagement. Decentralization in itself rarely shifts the existing balance of political power.

Under such (mundane) conditions, the design experiment offers some evidence that audio-visual technology can be used to ensure that the voices of the politically marginalized are at least heard in such forums. Clearly one of the lessons from the production and reception of the DVD is that it is vital to ensure that those filmed are politically marginalized! Short cuts taken by the Area Board managers in the production of the DVD (setting up interviews with known community activists) arguably undermined the overall impact of the intervention, increasing the hostility of already suspicious and uncomfortable elected representatives.

But this hostility was not just towards particular individuals on the DVD: elected representatives found uncomfortable the challenge that the voices on the DVD represented. In itself this may be a good thing: exposing the intransigence of existing political power holders. But it is not necessarily helpful in pushing forward the engagement agenda. Here the important issue is the capacity of the manager to facilitate the deliberations that interspersed the showing of sections of the DVD. The experiment cruelly exposed the limitations of a number of these managers. Facilitation to ensure inclusion is not an easy task. It is certainly not something that comes naturally to most people. And it is an undervalued element of participation exercises; a topic that receives negligible attention within democratic theory (Mansbridge, Hartz-Karp, Amengual and Gastil 2008; Smith 2009: 197–8). We may be able to create tools (such as the DVD) to bring the voice of the marginalized into debates, but the conditions need to be in place such that participants in the room are willing to take these tools – and the messages they convey – seriously. Creating a forum for participation is not enough: it must be well facilitated if it is to be effective. Further experimental research is needed to better understand the determinants of effective and inclusive democratic facilitation.

Finally the research reveals the challenging nature of design experiments. So much is out of the control of the research team: co-production of the experiment raises significant practical (and at times political) challenges. But the rewards of such research are potentially great. The next chapter takes a further look at how institutions do in fact respond when people choose to engage.

*Further reading*

Information on participatory video can be found at http://insightshare. org, where it is possible to download the book *Insights into Participatory Video: A Handbook for the Field*. The idea for the DVD intervention was to some extent influenced by the issue books produced for community meetings (or study circles) by the independent organization Everyday Democracy in the United States (http://www.everyday-democracy.org). Also see Improvement and Development Agency (IDeA) (2007), 'The political skills framework: a councillor's toolkit', London: IDeA, http:// www.idea.gov.uk/idk/aio/6515699. For more on the range of democratic innovations being institutionalized across the world, see *Beyond the Ballot* (Smith 2005), http://www.powerinquiry.org/publications/documents/ BeyondtheBallot_000.pdf and the user-generated platform *Participedia*, http://www.participedia.net.

# Linking

## Why institutions are critical for civic behaviour

If they are to be successful, nudge and think interventions need ways of linking citizens and political representatives in central and local government. Thinking makes more sense if the ideas that citizens come up with are reviewed, judged and preferably acted upon by policy-makers. It is also possible to imagine situations where nudges work better with links, too. Some of the nudges described in this volume aim to get people involved in making decisions jointly with decision-makers, or to petition, lobby or complain. Why participate if no one is listening?

The institutional links between citizens and government provide a framework for civic participation. Institutions have, in many cases, frustrated citizens' ability to be citizens, and therefore institutional reform is vital. While the experiments and other research in this volume suggest there is untapped citizen potential, this can be hard to realize from the ways in which institutions frame the debate, how they create structures and how they respond to citizens. Examples from everyday life are easy to come by: citizens can see where institutions promise choice and quality in public services but deliver long waits in doctors' waiting rooms, where their questions about rapidly changing populations have been suppressed, or that warnings about climate change come from the same politicians and civil servants who approve decisions to build new homes on flood plains. Nudge strategies are themselves premised on the idea that institutions could create stronger forms of citizenship if they dealt with people as they are, which is often more sympathetic or willing than institutions presume, but possibly less straightforwardly rational, more social and more emotional. Think strategies are a tool for debating how far institutional frameworks could, or should, intervene to shape people's behaviour, what choices citizens are willing to make or prepared to accept from governments. The issue is whether institutions can operate their frameworks for civic behaviour in a creative enough way to match the sophistication of citizens. Reform is extremely hard; some of the inherent characteristics of institutions arguably militate against reform.

Chapter 4 described some of the difficulties in persuading a public institution to tailor volunteering opportunities to better match citizens' preferences and interests. This chapter takes the discussion further, and looks at relationships between citizen groups and decision-makers within local institutions. We review existing evidence on the lack of responsiveness of institutions to citizens' attempts to be civic; then we look at how nudge and think can help develop more responsive institutions. We present an experiment on testing for the responsiveness of local councillors to a citizen-interest group lobby.

## Literature – what are the gaps in institutional responsiveness?

The literature on the quality of institutional framing makes for depressing reading. Broadly, since the mid-1960s, public trust in government and political institutions has been decreasing in all of the advanced industrialized democracies (Dalton 2004). Political trust is closely related to how far citizens feel institutions are accountable and respond to their needs and preferences. The Rockefeller Fund has a grant programme specifically designed to enhance institutional responsiveness because of perceived gaps (see http://www.rffund.org/responsiveness).

In the UK, the leaders of institutions misunderstand the needs and demands of citizens across a huge range of fundamental topics: citizens' preferred identities; preferences for participation in decision-making; citizens' preferences for where they live and with whom they share their neighbourhoods (Durose, Greasley and Richardson 2009). The culture of English local government has been described as: 'inward-looking, silo-based, resistant to change and challenge and more concerned with a self-serving attachment to a particular model of delivery than thinking what would produce the best outcome for people in the locality' (Improvement and Development Agency 2009: 8).

The public do not think local government is listening and responding to citizens' ideas; nor is it linking to concerns at the local level. Citizens and institutions need to be in dialogue with each other – or at least connect together – if institutions are to have a chance of responding to citizen views. Local political representatives are important to the public and seen as influential: in 2000, research showed that 66 per cent thought councillors were in charge of public services in their local area, and 65 per cent considered them to have the most influence on issues affecting their local area (Local Government Association 2008: 15). Despite this, in 2002, when asked, 26 per cent said they knew nothing at all about their local members; 65 per cent had never met any of their local councillors; and 61 per cent said they did not know the name of their local councillor (Local Government Association 2008: 14).

More importantly, the public do not trust local government to get on with making decisions effectively. They do not feel adequately represented, nor that local government is accountable; and they have not thought so for the last decade. For example, the 1998 British Social Attitudes Survey Local Government Module (Chivite-Matthews and Teal 2001) showed that 88 per cent said 'local councils would make better decisions if they made more effort to find out what local people want', and only 7 per cent felt 'local councillors should just get on and make the important decisions themselves. After all, that's what we elected them for'. A think strategy, such as a citizens' jury (described in the survey questionnaire as 12 to 15 'ordinary local people chosen at random'), was seen as able to make better decisions about the neighbourhood than local government would. Ten years on, a 2008 survey of public perceptions (Department for Communities and Local Government 2008: 20) showed that 38 per cent did not feel councillors were representative of their communities, 59 per cent did not believe that councillors adequately reflected their views, 62 per cent did not feel that they are given an adequate say in how local council services are run, and 92 per cent believed that councils could be more accountable.

Moreover, citizens believe local politicians to be out of touch, for example in 2004 (Department for Communities and Local Government 2007: 12–13) only 7 per cent of councillors thought they were out of touch with the public, compared to 43 per cent of the public who thought councillors were out of touch with the public. The study showed that 69 per cent of councillors believed they make decisions in touch with local views, whereas only 19 per cent of the public agreed. More worryingly, citizens felt that local councillors' behaviour had got worse between 2007 and 2009, and that local councillors were out for themselves, disrespectful and did not treat people equally (Standards for England 2009). Between 2007 and 2009, there was a rise of 4 per cent (from 28 to 32 per cent) in people saying all or most councillors use their political power for their own personal gain, and a fall in the percentage of people saying councillors work in interests of neighbourhood, with 29 per cent saying a few or none do in 2009 (Standards for England 2009: 8–9).

The systemic problems of the belief that experts know best have a knock-on effect for civic behaviour. Gerber and Phillips argue (from a US perspective) that:

When institutions are more responsive (i.e. when they produce policy outcomes that reflect the changing preferences of the median or some other important group of voters), political actors can achieve their policy goals within an existing institutional regime. When institutions are less responsive, some actors may prefer to circumvent status quo institutions and replace them with new ones. (Gerber and Phillips 2002: 2)

In 2008, a UK practitioner-developed framework on the ability of community groups to influence decision-making was produced after:

it became glaringly apparent to us that there was no point in focusing solely on 'developing;' communities which are empowered and empowering, if the agencies they are trying to connect with are shutting them out and behaving in disempowering ways. This stark realization kick-started the research [with] a focus on assessing and increasing public agencies' openness to influence. (Changes n.d.)

Some citizens are active despite a lack of responsiveness on the part of public authorities, and have high levels of motivation, or, some may argue, irrational behaviour. They could be described as persistent at the very least, given how little impact they feel they have through their unpaid activity. One research study (Newton, Pierce, Richardson and Williams 2010) showed that being civically active or engaged in public debate does not necessarily produce satisfied and empowered citizens who feel their efforts are taken seriously. The study showed that amongst people active in their communities, only a third (35 per cent) believed they could influence decisions, while 56 per cent of those who had been involved said that they could not, although this is higher than people who are not involved (35 per cent compared to 23 per cent) (Newton *et al.* 2010: 36). The main reason for these findings appears to be that people did not perceive changes to be happening as a result of their involvement, although we do not know whether these people started off more dissatisfied, and became involved in decision-making because they are already unhappy with decisions that had been made.

However, for some citizens, the marginal gains to be made from their potential involvement are off-putting enough to stop them becoming active. Other research shows that there is a feedback effect on civic attitudes and participation from poor responsiveness: 'The biggest deterrent to participation of all was citizens' perception – or experience – of a lack of council response to consultation' (Lowndes, Pratchett and Stoker 2001: 452). For larger jurisdictions, writers have argued that cross-national variations in political membership are not so much related to social or attitudinal differences between these countries' citizens, and are explained to a great extent by the structure of the political system of each nation (Morales 2009). In the United Kingdom, other evidence indicates a correlation between poor local government responsiveness and low levels of civic participation (Barnes, Stoker and Whiteley 2003). More responsive local authorities were correlated with higher levels of participation, although the direction of causation is unclear. The Newton *et al.* study examined the problem of making a causal inference in more detail, looking at why citizens did or did not feel they had influence over local decisions (Newton *et al.* 2010). Institutional responsiveness to citizens was critical, for example, to whether citizens felt that local public services acted on the concerns of local people. The study showed that 34 per cent of the variance of feelings of influence was explained by whether people felt that local public services acted on the concerns of local people (Newton *et al.* 2010: 31). Residents judged that local public institutions were responsive in several different ways: if they listened and heard what residents had to say; if they fed back on the outcomes of decisions; and if they made decisions people felt the majority agreed with. Feelings of influence were also linked to whether agencies had delivered on promises. Broken promises decreased trust in institutions.

## Links to nudge and think

An investigative audit of the practice of public authorities in engaging their citizens in local decision-making and consultative processes (Lowndes *et al.* 2006) identified the challenge of linking at the local level. The task was to ensure that formal and elected representatives draw upon the insights and understandings of a wide range of citizens. This research developed the diagnostic tool, CLEAR (discussed in Chapter 4). The implication of the argument is that participation is most effective when citizens have the resources to participate, are mobilized and enabled. Most importantly for our discussion on linking, the R in CLEAR stands for 'responded to':

> The 'responded to' factor is simultaneously the most obvious but also the most difficult factor in enhancing public participation. But it is also the factor most open to influence by public policy-makers. Leadership and decision-making arrangements – in political and managerial domains – play an important role in determining whether groups of

citizens are able to gain access to those with power, whether decision makers have a capacity to respond and whether certain groups are privileged over others in terms of the influence they exert. (Lowndes *et al.* 2006: 289)

Several of our experiments aimed to facilitate deliberation with citizens and to nudge citizens to behave more civically. But we did not want to ignore the institutional role. Our experiments were not premised on the idea that institutions were perfectly designed, with effective engagement structures and processes in place simply waiting for an apathetic citizenry to be mobilized into action. We understood that civic activity is a two-way process, and that people's negative experiences of engaging with the large, unwieldy and sometimes stubborn and paternal bureaucracies of power could have a significant part to play in their unwillingness to be mobilized. Could we turn the tables? What if similar nudge and think techniques could be applied to institutions to enhance their ability to respond?

## The experiment

The Building Links project tested out different ways that community organizations could approach local councillors, get their attention and win support for their work. How can both sides work together on relevant local issues and problems? How could citizen organizations lobby decision-makers? The aim was to see which, if any, was the more effective approach. We asked other questions. Do councillors find it hard to judge between different demands made on them? Can communities help with this by getting their message across more effectively?

The study was a randomized controlled trial, where the units were local politicians (councillors) in English local government. We recruited eight community groups, spread across the country in eight different local authorities. Each group had a real local issue they wanted to tackle, but all were keen to make stronger connections to their local councillors. We selected the authorities on the basis of the availability of a comparable and willing interest group to do the intervention, and actively recruited groups in different places in order to get variations in political control and location. The sample size was 248 councillors. This was based on a total of 496 councillors across all 8 local authorities in the experiment. We randomly selected half of the councillors in each authority to make up the sample, as we felt an approach to all councillors, in a round-robin style, would be counter-productive to our lobby.

The intervention was that each of the community groups sent letters to the randomly selected councillors in the sample in their local council. There were two differently worded letters, and each councillor received just one: that is, half the sample received letter A, and the other half got letter B, which meant that a quarter of all the councillors in that authority received each kind of letter. There was no control group, as the response from councillors not receiving a letter would have been difficult to measure. Both letters asked for help with the same problem, but one approach was based on the literature on how to campaign and lobby, and the other was not. Studies show there are several factors that contribute to an effective lobby, of which eight key ones are that:

1. the lobbying material comes from a credible source;
2. it frames the issue in a way that is consistent with lobbyists' values and goals;
3. it offers the policy-maker private or costly information that would otherwise be difficult for the policy-maker to gather;
4. it summarizes and processes a mass of publicly available information in a way that clarifies the implications for the policy-maker;
5. it contains emotive or symbolic appeals to commonly held values;
6. it outlines how current policy approaches lead to negative outcomes;
7. it outlines how an alternative approach would promote shared policy goals;
8. and it has a clear set of recommendations or makes a clearly articulated demand of the policy-maker.

The experiment incorporated the eight factors considered by the literature to form an effective lobbying letter. This created the two treatments: weak and strong. Letter A was designed to be the weak treatment. It contained weak, un-evidenced and not locally relevant versions of five of the eight factors in effective lobbying. It did not contain three of the eight factors. It had only one reference to a request, which was weak and unclear. Letter B was designed to be the strong treatment. It contained strong, evidenced and locally relevant versions of all the factors in effective lobbying. There were three references to a clear request and two references to all other factors.

We measured the results by (a) the number of replies to each of the two letters and (b) the helpfulness of the replies. Ultimately the best measure of quality would be that the lobby succeeded. Following the lobby, some of the groups saw progress, for example, a participatory arts organization was awarded a £0.25 million contract to provide services, and a carers network was invited to local authority strategic planning meetings for the first time. However, while positive for the groups, these outcome variables cannot be considered to be direct results of the intervention. Although concrete and observable outcomes like these are attractive for the research, they are decisions much further down the chain of decision-making and are the result of a complex mix of institutional factors not attributable solely to the treatment. A successful outcome to the lobby was not necessarily within the gift of all of the individual councillors.

The initial response by telephone, letter or email was used in the analysis as the outcome variable. Both treatments contained a set of generic requests as a basis for outcome measurement: 'We would very much appreciate the opportunity to collaborate. Please could you let us know: your position on [the relevant local issue]; and how you would like to take this issue forward?'

However, this causes an issue for the analysis of quality of response in that any verbal response to a request can be considered suspect. The analysis dealt with these issues by creating a coding framework that allowed for a series of different types of response from the same individual in order to see if a response was backed up by other (seemingly) helpful actions or comments, or if they were just empty phrases. A coding framework for the quality and content of the responses was created based on the generic request combined with the nature of the actual responses received. The coding framework covered: quality of help overall; a statement that the issue was not the councillor's responsibility or remit; the suggestion of other contacts without a direct referral; a direct referral to a civil servant/officer or relevant committee; a direct referral to a fellow councillor; willingness to take up the issue; the offer or occurrence of further discussion; a comment on the issue; an offer of personal support to the group for their lobby; willingness to meet or met in person; and the giving of information about party policy. The responses were then blind-coded by two researchers who had not been involved in the experiment and had no knowledge of which group the councillor was in.

## What did we find?

Overall, 18.5 per cent of councillors responded. There was a considerable variation according to local authority, ranging from 4.2 to 30.6 per cent. The weak letter, the one not based on the lobbying literature, had a slightly higher level of response and more helpful responses. The stronger letter based on the literature had a 16.0 per cent response. The more general letter based on the literature had a 21.0 per cent response. Therefore, the weak letter with its information-low and emotion-poor approach yielded a higher response – of 5 percentage points – than the strong letter with its information-high and emotion-rich approach. The difference is not statistically significant, however, and the conclusion must be that the type of letter did not make a difference in the replies overall.

The number of responses is only one outcome. The quality of the responses is also clearly critical; fewer but constructive and supportive responses from appropriate decision-makers may be of more benefit to the interest groups than a larger number of non-committal or unhelpful answers from politicians not in a position to assist. Using the data from the qualitative coding of the helpfulness of the replies, we probed the structure of these responses with factor analysis (a statistical procedure that reduces a large number of responses to a few common factors). Helpful responses included councillors expressing a willingness to meet, and offering face-to-face follow-up discussions, or positively signposting the lobbyist on to colleagues if the issue would be better dealt with by someone else. Less helpful and dismissive responses included councillors stating it was not their remit or responsibility and the letter writer needed to go elsewhere, without positively signposting the lobbyist on to colleagues or referring them elsewhere, or even, in many cases, offering a relevant name to the writer. The regression analysis (see Richardson and John 2011) shows that the extent to which people passed the letter on to another person in the council was more influenced by the better letter than the one with less information.

## Conclusion

The core idea we were testing was that decision-makers within public institutions could be nudged to be more responsive. Our nudge was to present local politicians with a lobby from groups they were largely unaware of, and that did not have relationships with councillors. The strong letter was information-rich, and attempted to offer politicians with intelligence not only on the salience of the local issue to be tackled, but also information about the legitimacy of the community group and their potential contribution to joint problem-solving with the local authority. This was based on a wide and robust literature, which indicated that informational lobbying was an effective tactic. Unfortunately, this was not the case in our experiment. What is also striking is that there was no difference between the supposedly weaker and stronger letters. What is also noticeable is the low level of response to either of the letters from community groups. These groups were lobbying their locally elected representatives to seek their help on what they see as a genuine local issue.

Indeed, follow-up research talking directly to councillors shows that they suffer from information overload, and find it hard to manage demands made on them. Demands on local politicians have substantially increased in the last decade. Another possible explanation of the responses may be that a rise in the number of internal organizational and party political demands has left less time to represent the people who voted them in, or process lobbying requests from unknown bodies. It suggests that UK local politicians may still be suffering from a perception of themselves as having weak status and low power. This might also explain our other finding, that the treatment encouraged politicians to pass the letter on to another person, possibly of higher status, in the council.

Some preliminary follow-up research for this project has been finding that local councillors do feel overwhelmed by irrelevant paperwork and demands, and unable to influence their own bureaucracies in order to create change. However, this does not take away from the fact that so few replied, whether to dismiss the claim being made on them, to request a less cognitively demanding letter or even to explain the limitations they faced. Under these circumstances it is hard for the community groups doing the lobbying not to feel that their institutions do not value them and their contributions.

The literature, and our experiment, reveals the extent of the gap between citizens and local representatives but also how hard it will be to close that gap. It maybe that weaknesses in linking show the limited possibilities of both nudge and think strategies – as effective policies need citizens to feed back to decisions. The evidence indicates some urgent work, such as training, is needed to develop the capacity of local elected members as community leaders. It suggests that more work is needed to build relationships between community organizations and local members. Local authorities could manage their communications with councillors to allow members to focus on their priorities.

Beyond these small-scale local practical measures, there is a bigger challenge: how to address the more fundamental cultural and organizational framing issues. The process of engaging citizens needs to be complemented with a reform of government to make those in power better able to listen to and work with citizens and community groups. This is particularly critical at the level of local government, where the people who are seen by the citizens as decision-makers feel very disempowered themselves.

*Further reading*
There are few experimental studies of lobbying, and most were unpublished at the time of writing. See Grose, C.R. and Russell, C.A. (2009), 'Avoiding the Vote: A Theory and Field Experiment the Social Costs of Public Participation', Working paper, Nashville, TN: Vanderbilt University; Butler, D.M. and Broockman, D.E. (2009), 'Who Helps DeShawn Register to Vote? A Field Experiment on State Legislators', Working paper, New Haven, CT: Yale University. Also of relevance is Chin, M.L. Bond, J.R. and Geva, N. (2000), 'A Foot in the Door: An Experimental Study of PAC and Constituency Effects on Access', *Journal of Politics*, 62: 534–49.

# Conclusion:
# Experimenting with Ways
# to Change Civic Behaviour

In this book we have tried to find out how public agencies can encourage citizens to contribute more to society. We have examined a wide range of activities through which citizens can make that contribution including voting, volunteering, petitioning, taking part in debates on policy issues, recycling and donating. We have detailed a similarly broad range of interventions that public agencies and other bodies can carry out such as canvassing, giving feedback, making direct requests of citizens, involving them in debate and inviting them to make pledges. We have used research tools of the highest quality – randomized controlled trials and design experiments – to test our claims. We have provided evidence of what works and of what works better. With this evidence at their fingertips, policy-makers are equipped to select effective interventions that involve citizens in public life and as a result improve policy outcomes.

We build on a body of work by the many academics who have argued that citizens are central to public policy-making and implementation. Hirst was prescient: he made the case for associative democracy as an alternative to more state-controlled forms of rule (Hirst 1993). Citizens are able to participate in locally based associations, which can sustain a more decentralized pattern of politics. Scholars working on research with the label social capital have also stressed the positive role that individuals play in forming beneficial social networks. Clusters of social capital play a role in sustaining positive policy outcomes and maintaining the quality of government (Putnam 1993; Putnam 2000). Halpern, in his review of the literature, assembled a large amount of observational evidence, finding that there is such a relationship between social networks/trust and desired policy outcomes occurring across many policy fields, such as crime, health and education (Halpern 2005). His later book argues that societies have a large amount of hidden wealth in the form of stocks of social cooperation and intelligence, which policy-makers can tap into if only they know how to (Halpern 2010).

In addition to the more general treatises, there have been many case studies of how policy might be improved by involving the citizen more.

Fung, for example, examined the participation experiments of cities in the US whereby citizens have sought to use new decision-making forums to influence the political agenda and to achieve social policy objectives such as the reduction of crime (Fung 2003b; Fung 2006). Brannan, John and Stoker brought together the evidence from a selection of policies in the UK that involve the citizen directly, such as tenant initiatives and crime on housing estates (Brannan *et al.* 2006). They found that citizen action can – in the right circumstances – overcome the bias of institutions that often limit political and civic participation. Sirianni made a cogent argument for involving citizens in a new partnership with state institutions (Sirianni 2009). He provided many examples of collaborative governance from the United States, and develops a set of principles policy-makers could follow. Smith reviewed the evidence about democratic innovations that have emerged across the world, and which shows the many varieties of these experiments, such as participatory budgeting, citizens' assemblies and experiments in e-democracy (Smith 2009). Richardson collected examples from a hundred community groups of Do-It-Yourself community action in the UK, showing how citizens can deliver interventions themselves without much help from government (Richardson 2008).

These reviews and studies – often using valuable research designs, such as case studies or analyses of observational data – have provided persuasive arguments that there is potential for citizen mobilization. But in our view they lack the killer evidence to make their cases compelling, particularly concerning what government and other agencies can do to foster change. In this volume we offer our own unique solution to this problem: randomized controlled trials. They can provide conclusive evidence of what works because of their ability to demonstrate convincingly whether an intervention was successful or not, and because they provide the genuine counterfactual of what would have happened without the intervention. The trials we have presented in this book show what is possible. Added to this we have insights from our two more qualitative studies – design experiments – which we used to examine more intensive and complex interventions (see the Appendix for the summary of the methods of the experiments).

Our message is that public interventions do make a difference. All our experiments worked – to a greater or lesser extent – in stimulating civic behaviour and/or changing attitudes. There is much that public agencies can do to get citizens involved with policy. We believe that citizens are willing to do more and they do not need that much encouragement to get there. We are aware of the constraints in increasing participation that many critics have pointed out. We know that a small minority of citizens do most of the volunteering, and many of these people live in affluent areas (Mohan 2011). Most people either lack the interest or the capacity to get involved. It is true we found that more affluent areas were more susceptible to our experiments, such as the book donation experiment (Chapter 7), but we also found that poorer areas responded positively as well. In our volunteering experiment (Chapter 4) we found that people from a range of backgrounds came forward. We uncovered a similarly diverse set of responses to our invention in our recycling experiments (Chapter 3). Contrary to usual expectations, we found the canvassing campaign was more successful in the most deprived neighbourhoods and those places that have a large ethnic minority population.

Conventional methods of recruitment often tend to deploy the personal social networks of activists. These people often recruit people similar to themselves. If public organizations bypass these networks and ask randomly selected people directly, unsurprisingly we get a more representative group of participants. Indeed, a study of new forms of participation (John 2009) found that citizen governance forums, in contrast to the traditional political activities of petitioning and protest, tend to recruit participants who are younger and are members of ethnic minorities. Similar evidence has been uncovered concerning participation in other forms of carefully designed democratic innovations (Smith 2009). In short, in spite of the constraints on expanding social and political participation, there is much that government can do to involve citizens from a wider social background than the ones who already take part in existing forms of civic involvement.

With our experiments testing out nudge and think, we found that the nudge experiments, on the whole, worked. We could knock on citizens' doors to encourage people to recycle their household waste and to vote in elections (Chapters 3 and 5); we could give them feedback too on how well they are doing so as to encourage even greater recycling of their food waste (Chapter 3). When citizens are given due credit for their contribution, we can get them to pledge to make donations to charity (Chapter 7). Critically for the nudge approach, we found that mandated choice works almost as well as opting out (Chapter 8). Defaults work just as Thaler and Sunstein say they do (Thaler and Sunstein 2008). As a result we can say to policy-makers that they have a set of information-based tools of government that structure how citizens receive a signal or a cue, and can encourage them to volunteer, participate in politics or do good in the community.

Nudge is, of course, not a panacea. The first issue is that nudge interventions tend to have weak effects, which is not particularly surprising because these interventions are light-touch in character. So the experiments show an uplift of participation of between 1 and 9 percentage points. This falls short of the transformation of public policy outcomes that many might see as essential for dealing with current policy problems. On the other hand, the nudges are relatively cheap to implement. Our local nudges cost about £10,000 to administer, which is a small amount of money even in an age of fiscal austerity, and turns into a reasonable cost for each extra item of waste recycled, books donated, organs promised and so on. Even the larger experiments were not very expensive, such as the online donations experiment at £22,000. The online deliberation was more expensive at £100,000, but this was a national sample and represented our commitment to investigate think as much as we investigated nudge.

It could also be argued that if governments were to provide some of the nudges themselves, and with more institutional or rule-based changes alongside the information provision, we might expect a much larger effect. But – and this is the second limitation (or advantage depending how one sees it) – the nudger needs to be believed and this is a constraint in an era of large-scale distrust of government and public officials. Nudges work precisely because government is not so directly involved. People trust a message when it is from a reliable third-party source rather than from government itself. One of the ironies of our findings is that policy-makers can learn from our work that nudges are effective but also that they may find it hard to nudge by themselves. Public officials may find it advantageous to work with other partners in delivering nudge interventions at a local level. Such local experiments can complement a nationally rolled out programme. They show how innovations can work best when government is at one step removed from the general public and is not nudging them individually.

The third limitation is that the range of possible interventions may be limited to those aspects of behaviour where people have already made up their minds and are willing to act. This may leave out a range of other behaviours that are more controversial and that may require a great deal more effort to change. Examples are recycling, which is already widely perceived as a good thing to do, and organ donation; the issue in these cases is that while most people agree with the ideas of recycling and organ donation, many do not take action. This gap becomes even more important when the nudges address issues of public controversy and require citizens to engage in larger and more profound changes than the ones with which we presented them. This provides a justification to our use of think, which may be appropriate precisely in those contexts where there is not a settled point of view.

It is likely that nudge may not have a long-term effect and this is its fourth limitation. Certainly we do find that people learn how to change behaviour and observe a downstream effect. There is an effect through habit, but this decays over time. In the Get Out the Vote study it did so by as much as 50 per cent, and there was a similar level of fall-off in the canvassing/recycling intervention. Of course, this criticism needs to be considered fairly. All interventions have a time-limited nature, so the effectiveness of nudges needs to be assessed alongside the effectiveness of other interventions, such as public funding, for example, which also reduces in impact once the investment has been made (such as with an urban regeneration project). The mistake in our view would be to see the nudge being undertaken in isolation from other policies and without considering the views of citizens themselves. As we argue below, nudges work best when seen as part of the local policy process – part of the necessary interaction between policy-makers and citizens. This would imply that nudges should be repeated and varied by these local agencies, as they learn from experience. And it was this creative process of using nudges that our design experiments attempted to reproduce. In this way, the time-limited nature of nudges is not a disadvantage because public agencies and other partners are continually using a wide range of time-limited strategies to improve public policy.

The fifth limitation stems from the collaboration needed to implement nudges involving public agencies. The messiness of everyday policy-implementation means that it takes a lot of effort to get a nudge off the ground, to get partners to work together and to get the details right. Not all of our nudges worked in all respects, as we saw with the volunteering design experiment using a call centre (see Chapter 4). This is the real world of policy implementation, which can be very distant from the pronouncements of government or the mission statements of glossy white papers. This very messiness, however, should not be seen as a disadvantage, but it can be used to harness local energy and enthusiasm, as we explain below.

The limitations to nudge should not be used to decry our results – far from it. But they should encourage policy-makers to think about the appropriate conditions for introducing nudges, to know when and where they are going to be effective, perhaps alongside other interventions. The limitations also argue for a potentially more profound information tool to be considered, one that might lead to more long-term, systematic changes in citizen behaviour. This tool is discussion and deliberation – what we call think. Our results show considerable potential for this institutional reform. For example, the design experiment in Wiltshire with councillors (see Chapter 10) demonstrates that you can introduce into local government forums the voices of those who do not usually participate and this can shift the perceptions of those involved. The online experiment (Chapter 9) shows that you can engage large numbers of people on controversial topics such as youth anti-social behaviour and the implications of greater ethnic diversity of neighbourhoods. They are able to debate these issues without recrimination and without falling out.

But there are some limitations to think, too. First, think can fail when it asks people to engage in the more tricky moral choices. With organ donation, when people were asked to deliberate as well as being nudged, there was a weaker effect than produced by the nudge alone. The process of deliberation appeared to firm up participants' doubts, if nothing else. This could be a good thing if reflection is the goal, but the assumption that further thought will lead automatically to the policy-maker's desired end needs careful consideration.

The other limitation is that the newest form of citizen interaction, the internet, may not be the best medium to encourage the majority of citizens to change their attitudes, although those who selected into the youth anti-social behaviour debates did change their views (see Chapter 9). The attitudes of many remained the same in spite of people being willing to sign into an experiment, being presented with information about these controversial and topical issues, having the chance to post their own views and to see the posts of others. It might be said that perhaps our intervention was not strong enough – that there was not enough on the discussion forum for citizens to engage in or that it did not have the potential to transform citizens. It may be the case that deliberating online can be challenging because of the nature of the online environment, which means that participants are not forced to pay attention to information and it is more difficult to encourage exchanges of views. The big attraction of the online environment is the number of people it can engage, but there needs to be greater effort in the design of online interventions to make them more fully deliberative exercises. In fact, we believe that our online deliberation has as many lessons for nudge as for think by highlighting the importance of institutional design, which can encourage citizens to be mutually respectful, even when debating controversial policies and issues. It is possible that pro-civic behaviour cues can be built into the design of online discussion forums.

In the short term there is a better case for using the internet as a site for nudge than for delivering think interventions. Our experiment on e-petitions achieved a significant shift in behaviour with much less of an intervention than the deliberation (see Chapter 6). The e-petition participants simply saw the number of other people participating, in what must be have been an almost subliminal experience compared to the vast number of videos, links to information posts and email reminders we offered in the online deliberation. The design possibilities of the internet and the large numbers of users involved allow policy-makers to make minor modifications to the design of the interface between the citizen and the state – for example in providing feedback and in framing information – and to expect significant behaviour change as a result of these nudges. With the current level of technology and its increasing use, the potential of the internet for both nudge and think has yet to be tapped.

But in spite of the online revolution, face-to-face interventions still have traction, both for think and nudge. Thus, many of our interventions were old-fashioned in their method of delivery. Consider doorstep-canvassing, for instance, as used with our voting (Chapter 5) and recycling experiments (Chapter 3). This gets results through the personal touch of the canvasser meeting face-to-face with a local resident. Deliberation in a community setting in Wiltshire delivered positive outcomes too (Chapter 10). Even when not face-to-face, the same effect can be achieved by talking to potential volunteers on the telephone – as we found in our call centre experiment (Chapter 4). Reading a printed booklet was an effective nudge in our student organ donation experiment (Chapter 8), an old-fashioned kind of intervention compared to the internet posts and blogs we created. Moreover, the other ancient form of communication of getting a letter in the post is also powerfully effective in reaching a large range of citizens, as we found in our book donation experiment (Chapter 7) and our feedback intervention on food waste (Chapter 3). This is especially important as there is no national database of email addresses and not everyone has access to the internet. In spite of the valuable results we achieved in our online deliberation and organ donation experiments, we cannot routinely rely on survey companies to collect names for us, as we did for those experiments. In the end, that group was a self-selected minority of people who gave their names to be on survey lists. Thus, a range of techniques is needed to deliver nudge and think, with each one having its advantages and disadvantages.

Overall, we think policy-makers need to recognize that nudging and thinking are complex processes, and context may be the factor that determines where one may be appropriate and not the other. We think that policy interventions could use elements of both nudge and think, partly because they resemble each other. If done in a sensitive manner, both can involve some reflection and some debate, even if that is limited as it was in our doorstep-canvassing experiment, where citizens wanted to have a conversation with the canvassers while they were being nudged. Many of our nudges (and some of our thinks) took place in a local context, where third-sector parties and local government itself were willing to engage with experiments. Deciding what to nudge and implementing it can involve much discussion and think, as does examining reaction to the nudges and responding to the lessons learned with new local policies. This form of local interaction was built into our design experiments, such as the call centre and decentralization experiments, but also affected how we delivered and reported nudges over recycling and donations. In this way, a devolved and locally appropriate version of nudge, where the intervention becomes part of the learning process and where there is sufficient decentralization of power, allows a range of actors to shape local policy-making – citizens, local associations, the third sector and local government all play a role.

Looking at it this way we can challenge one of the biggest criticisms of nudge – that it takes away citizen freedom by being manipulative – a charge that is levelled because nudge is thought to work at subliminal level rather than in the open process of democratic debate (Anderson 2010). Nudge may even be criticized as another instance of the nanny or bossy state which is keen to tell citizens what to do without allowing much reflection or reaction from citizens themselves. An extreme version of nudge would see a central agency collecting all the evidence, a nudge version of the National Institute for Clinical Excellence reviewing many hundreds of trials and then rolling out nudge interventions across the country, and in so doing implementing a science of behaviour change. We do not subscribe to this vision – we think there is a more locally focused alternative where public agencies and citizen-based organizations can experiment with interventions and can judge what is best for their local area. In this way, the nudge and think can coexist together in more localized and experimental political culture and practice.

Seen in this way, nudge and think help drive change at a local level. But we are not naive about the structural obstacles to achieving social change, given social inequalities in British society and its neighbourhoods. But our experiments show that interventions tailored in the right way can partially overcome some of the obstacles. We strongly believe that the reform agenda of civic engagement using nudging and think cannot be brushed aside by reference to citizen apathy or the inevitable inequalities of political participation. In fact, our positive results and broad base of involvement point in the opposite direction.

The big question, in our view, is whether central and local public agencies are ready to respond to the energy of citizen-based activism. A locally based nudge-think experimental culture in public agencies implies that they, too, respond to signals from citizens themselves as well producing them. But we had some indication that it may be public authorities that are at fault rather than apathetic or unwilling citizens. In three of our experiments, we found it was elected officials or bureaucrats that provided the main obstacles to change. In the phone experiment when citizens called to make a complaint to the council (Chapter 4), we asked them to volunteer. We found the citizens were willing, but the council could not find them appropriate things to do and so these potential volunteers gave up. In Wiltshire, it was the councillors who reacted badly to hearing the voice of the excluded in their local board meetings (Chapter 10). Similarly, we found in our lobby experiment that less than one in five councillors responded to a community lobby, which was well reasoned and on a matter of local interest (Chapter 11). If the politicians and bureaucrats are not going to respond to citizen concerns, what is the point in stimulating citizens to get more involved? In this sense, it is the policy-makers as much as the citizens who should be nudged and who need to learn how to think.

# Appendix: Note on Results from the Experiments

This appendix provides a summary of the results from our experiments. Differences in the unit of analysis and study design prevent a uniform measure of effect size, which may be comparable across the interventions. However, these figures summarize the percentage shifts the intervention achieved or give a qualitative assessment in the case of the design experiments.

**Table A1.1** Effects of the experiments

| Chapter & Topic | Intervention | Effect of the intervention in comparison to a control group | Nudge or Think |
|---|---|---|---|
| **Chapter 3** Recycling experiment 1 (household recycling) | Canvassing | Recycling increased by 5% (immediate), drops to a 4% increase (3 months later) | Nudge |
| Recycling experiment 2 (food waste) | Feedback | Recycling increased by 3% | Nudge |
| **Chapter 4** Volunteering | Asking | Initial surge of interest but no change in volunteering levels | Nudge |
| **Chapter 5** Voting | i) Telephone calls ii) Canvassing | i) 3.5% more votes ii) 3.6% more votes | Nudge |
| **Chapter 6** Petitioning | Social information | i) 9% more petitions signed in lab study ii) 5.2% more petitions signed field study | Nudge |
| **Chapter 7** Giving (books) | i) Pledging ii) Pledging & Publicity | i) 0.9% more donations (non-significant) ii) 1.6% more donations | Nudge |
| **Chapter 8** Organ donating experiment 1 (information & discussion) | i) Information ii) Information & Discussion | i) Registrations increased by 4% ii) Registrations decreased by 15% | Nudge v. Nudge & Think |
| Organ donating experiment 2 (choice architecture) | i) Presumed consent ii) Mandated choice | i) Registrations increased by 8% ii) Registrations increased by 5% | Nudge & Think |
| **Chapter 9** Debating (online experiment) | i) Discussion forums & information ii) Information only | i) Modest opinion shifts in policy preferences; no changes in policy knowledge ii) No change | Think |
| **Chapter 10** Including (DVD) | DVD portraying views of politically disengaged groups | Discussions with DVD generated debate, where decision-makers were more considerate of disengaged groups; DVDs influenced Area Boards' thinking about future engagement but created some resistance amongst councillors | Think |
| **Chapter 11** Linking (letters to councillors) | i) Weak letter ii) Strong letter | i) 21% response from councillors ii) 16% response from councillors (no control group in this study) | Nudge |

# Glossary

*Behavioural economics*: A branch of economics that stresses the cognitive influences and limits on human behaviour. By stressing the use of judgement and heuristics, it is thought to depart from the classic rational model of decision-making.

*Control group*: One of the groups randomized as part of a randomized controlled trial. The control group does not get the intervention so may be used a base from which to compare the impact of the intervention in the treatment group.

*Counterfactual*: A piece of information or inference that shows what would have happened in the absence of an intervention or event.

*Experiment*: A method of research where the people or the area receiving the intervention or treatment is randomly different from a control group or between treatment groups. This includes natural experiments and randomized controlled trials.

*External validity*: The extent to which research findings may be generalized to other cases.

*Hawthorne effect*: The impact on the results of research caused by an adjustment or improvement in the behaviour of people because they are being studied.

*Inference*: Asserting a relationship between two variables.

*Internal validity*: The extent to which research findings represent the actual causal relationship.

*Interrupted time series*: A method for finding out whether a population, or an area that gets an intervention, improves when compared to a comparison group. It performs time series analysis on the two groups to see if one group's outcomes change at the point of, or shortly after, the intervention.

*Intervention*: The means by which an agency seeks to change behaviour or outcomes in a population. In an experiment, the treatment group receives the intervention.

*Observational data*: Data collected through observing the subjects of interest rather than from an experiment that seeks to manipulate the outcomes.

*Significant*: A shorthand for statistically significant, that is that the researcher can be confident with a minimum level of risk (5 per cent) that an independent variable affects a dependent variable in a regression, or there is an association or correlation between two variables in a table.

*Randomized controlled trial*: An experiment where the units of observation are randomized into two or more groups with one as the control group and the others as the treatment group or groups, or randomized between treatment groups.

*Selection bias*: A natural human process whereby some people or units select into an intervention and some do not, which means the results may be biased when making an inference to the population, possibly leading to an overestimate of the effectiveness of interventions.

*Treatment group*: One of the groups randomized as part of a randomized controlled trial. The treatment group gets the intervention so may be used to compare values of the control group or another treatment group so as to evaluate its impact.

# References

Abadie, A. and Gay, S. (2006), 'The Impact of Presumed Consent Legislation on Cadeveric Organ Donation: A Cross-Country Study', *Journal of Health Economics*, 25: 599–620.

Abers, R. (2000), *Inventing Local Democracy: Grassroots Politics in Brazil*, Boulder, CO, and London: Lynne Rienner.

Ackerman, B. and Fishkin, J. (2004), *Deliberation Day*, New Haven, CT: Yale University Press.

Agur, M. and Low, N. (2009), *2007–08 Citizenship Survey: Empowered Communities Topic Report*, London: Department for Communities and Local Government.

Anderson, J. (2010), 'Review: Richard Thaler and Cass Sunstein: *Nudge: Improving Decisions about Health, Wealth, and Happiness*', *Economics and Philosophy*, 26: 389–406.

Ariely, D., Bracha, A. and Meier, S. (2009), 'Doing Good or Doing well? Image Motivation and Monetary Incentives in Behaving Prosocially', *American Economic Review*, 99: 544–55.

Askew, R., John, P. and Liu, H. (2010), 'Can Policy Makers Listen to Researchers? An Application of the Design Experiment Methodology to a Local Drugs Policy Intervention', *Policy and Politics*, 38: 583–98.

Barber, B. (1998), 'Three Scenarios for the Future of Technology and Strong Democracy', *Political Quarterly*, 113: 573–89.

Barnes, M., Stoker, G. and Whiteley, P. (2003), *Developing Civil Renewal: Some Lessons From Research*, ESRC Seminar Series, Swindon: ESRC.

Bator, R. and Cialdini, R. (2000), 'The Application of Persuasion Theory to the Development of Effective Proenvironmental Public Service Announcements', *Journal of Social Issues*, 56: 527–41.

Baumgartner, F.R. and Jones, B.D. (1993), *Agendas and Instability in American Politics*, Chicago, IL: University of Chicago Press.

Benkler, Y. (2006), *The Wealth of Networks: How Social Production Transforms Markets and Freedom*, New Haven, CT: Yale University Press.

Best, S.J., Krueger, B. and Ladewig, J. (2007), 'The Effect of Risk Perceptions on Online Political Participatory Decisions', *Journal of Information Technology and Politics*, 4: 5–17.

Beveridge, W. (1948), *Voluntary Action: A Report on Methods of Social Advance*, London: George Allen and Unwin.

Bimber, B. (2003), *Information and American Democracy: Technology in the Evolution of Political Power*, Cambridge: Cambridge University Press.

Brannan, T., John, P. and Stoker, G. (eds) (2006), *Re-energizing Citizenship: Strategies for Civil Renewal*, Basingstoke: Palgrave Macmillan.

Boyle, D. and Harris, M. (2009), *The Challenge of Co-Production*, London: Nesta.

Braybrooke, D. and Lindblom, C. (1963), *A Strategy of Decision*, New York, NY: Free Press.

British Medical Association (2008), 'BMA Briefing Paper – Presumed Consent For Organ Donation, UK', *Medical News Today*, 14 November.

Brown, A. (1992), 'Design Experiments: Theoretical and Methodological Challenges in Creating Complex Interventions in Classroom Settings', *Journal of the Learning Sciences*, 2: 141–78.

Bryce, W., Day, R. and Olney, T. (1997), 'Commitment Approach to Motivating Community Recycling: New Zealand Kerbside Trial', *Journal of Consumer Affairs*, 31: 27–52.

Burn, S.M. and Oskamp, S. (1986), 'Increasing Community Recycling with Persuasive Communication and Public Commitment', *Journal of Applied Social Psychology*, 16: 29–41.

Butler, D.M. and Broockman, D.E. (2009), 'Who Helps DeShawn Register to Vote? A Field Experiment on State Legislators', Working paper, New Haven, CT: Yale University.

Cabannes, Y. (2004), 'Participatory Budgeting: A Significant Contribution to Participatory Democracy', *Environment and Urbanization*, 16: 27–46.

Cabinet Office (2003), *The Magenta Book: Guidance Notes for Policy Evaluation and Analysis*, London: Cabinet Office, http://www.policyhub. gov.uk/magenta_book [accessed 16 May 2011].

Cabinet Office (Halpern, D., Bates, C., Mulgan, G. and Aldridge, S. with Beales, G. and Heathfield, A.) (2004), *Personal Responsibility and Changing Behaviour: The State of its Knowledge and its Implications for Public Policy*, London: Cabinet Office.

Cederman, L.-E. and Kraus, P.A. (2005), 'Transnational Communication and the European Demos, in R. Latham and S. Sassen (eds), *Digital Formations: IT and New Architectures in the Global Realm*, Princeton, NJ: Princeton University Press.

Changes (n.d.), 'Community Empowerment stories', http://changesuk.net/ themes/community-empowerment/stories [accessed 16 May 2011]

Chin, M.L., Bond, J.R. and Geva, N. (2000), 'A Foot in the Door: An Experimental Study of PAC and Constituency Effects on Access', *Journal of Politics*, 62: 534–49.

Chivite-Matthews, N.I. and Teal, J. (2001), *1998 British Social Attitudes Survey: Secondary Data Analysis of the Local Government Module*, London: Department of the Environment, Transport and the Regions.

Choi, J., Laibson, D., Madrian, B. and Metrick, A. (2003), 'Optimal Defaults', *American Economic Review*, 93: 180–85.

Cialdini, R.B. (2007), *Influence. The Psychology of Persuasion*, New York, NY: Collins Business.

Cialdini, R.B. (2009), *Influence: Science and Practice*, Needham Heights, MA: Allyn and Bacon.

Clarke, H., Kornberg, A., McIntyre, C., Bauer-Kaase, P. and Kaase, M. (1999), 'The Effect of Economic Priorities on the Measurement of Value Change', *American Political Science Review*, 93: 637–47.

Cobb, P., Confrey, J., diSessa, A., Lehrer, R. and Schauble, L. (2003), 'Design Experiments in Educational Research' in A. Kelly (ed.), *Educational Researcher*, 32: 9–13.

Coleman, S. (2004), 'Connecting Parliament to the Public via the Internet: Two Case Studies of Online Consultations', *Information, Communication and Society*, 7: 1–22.

Collins, A. (1992), 'Towards a Design Science of Education', in E. Scanlon and T. O'Shea (eds), *New Directions in Educational Technology*, Berlin: Springer Verlag.

Collins. A., Joseph, D. and Bielaczyc, K. (2004), 'Design Research: Theoretical and Methodological Issues', *Journal of the Learning Sciences*, 13: 15–42.

Corporation for National and Community Service (2006) *Volunteering in America 2006: National, State, and City Information*, Washington, DC: Corporation for National and Community Service.

Corporation for National and Community Service (2010), *Volunteering in America 2010: National, State, and City Information*, Washington, DC: Corporation for National and Community Service.

Cotterill. S. and Richardson, L. (2010), 'Expanding the Use of Experiments on Civic Behavior: Experiments with Local Governments as Research Partners', *Annals of the American Academy of Political and Social Science*, 628: 148–64.

Cotterill, S., John, P., Liu, H. and Nomura, H. (2009), 'Mobilizing Citizen Effort to Enhance Environmental Outcomes: A Randomised Controlled Trial of a Door-to-Door Recycling Campaign', *Journal of Environmental Management*, 91: 403–10.

Cotterill, S., John, P. and Richardson, L. (2010), 'The Impact of a Pledge Campaign and the Promise of Publicity on Charitable Giving: A Randomised Controlled Trial of a Book Donation Campaign', paper presented to the Randomised Controlled Trials in the Social Sciences Conference, York, September 2010.

Cronqvist, H. and Thaler, R. (2004), 'Design Choices in Privatised Social-Security Systems: Learning From the Swedish Experience', *American Economic Review*, 94: 424–8.

Cutts, D., Fieldhouse, E. and John, P. (2009), 'Is Voting Habit Forming? The Longitudinal Impact of a GOTV Campaign in the UK', *Journal of Elections Public Opinion and Parties*, 19: 251–63.

Dahlberg, L. (2007), 'Rethinking the Fragmentation of the Cyberpublic: From Consensus to Contestation', *New Media and Society*, 9: 827–47.

Dalton, R. (2004), *Democratic Challenges, Democratic Choices: The Erosion of Political Support in Advanced Industrial Democracies*, Oxford: Oxford University Press.

Das-Gupta, I. (2008), 'Volunteer Schemes 'Not Effective'', *Third Sector Online*, 9 January 8, http://www.thirdsector.co.uk/news/archive/775360/ Volunteer-schemes-not-effective [accessed 16 May 2011].

Dawney, E. and Shah, H. (2005), *Behavioural Economics: Seven Principles for Policy Makers*, London: New Economics Foundation.

Department for Communities and Local Government (2007), *Representing the Future: The Report of the Councillors Commission*, London: Department for Communities and Local Government.

Department for Communities and Local Government (2008), *Communities in Control: Real People, Real Power*, Cm. 742, Norwich: The Stationery Office.

Department for Communities and Local Government (2009), *Citizenship Survey: 2009–10 (April–June 2009), England Statistical Release*, 9, London: Department for Communities and Local Government.

Department of Health (2008), *Organs for Transplants. A Report from the Organ Donation Taskforce*, London: Department of Health.

diSessa, A. (1991), 'Local Sciences: Viewing the Design of Human-Computer Systems as Cognitive Science', in J. Carroll (ed.), *Designing Interaction: Psychology at the Human-Computer Interface*, New York, NY: Cambridge University Press.

Docter, S. and Dutton, W. (1998), 'The First Amendment Online: Santa Monica's Public Electronic Network', in R. Tsagarousianou, D. Tambini and C. Bryan (eds), *Cyberdemocracy: Technologies, Cities and Civic Networks*, London: Routledge.

Dolan, P., Hallsworth, M., Halpern, D. and King, D. (2010), *Mindspace: Influencing Behaviour Through Public Policy*, London: Institute for Government.

Druckman, J., Green, D., Kuklinski, J. and Lupia, A. (2006), 'The Growth and Development of Experimental Research in Political Science', *American Political Science Review*, 100: 627–36.

Dunleavy, P., Margetts, H., Bastow, S. and Tinkler, J. (2006), *Digital Era Governance: IT Corporations, the State, and E-government*, Oxford: Oxford University Press.

Durose, C., Greasley, S. and Richardson, L. (eds) (2009), *Changing Local Governance, Changing Citizens*, Bristol: Policy Press.

EOS Gallop Europe (2002), *Flash Eurobarometer 135: Internet and the Public at Large*, Brussels: EOS Gallop Europe.

Eurotransplant (2006), *Key Facts and Figures on EU Organ Donation and Transplantation*, Brussels: European Union Directorate-General for Health and Consumers/Europe for Patients.

Fabre, J. (1998), 'Organ Donation and Presumed Consent', *The Lancet*, 352: 150.

Farsides, T. (2007), 'The Psychology of Altruism', *The Psychologist*, 20: 474–7.

Fearon, J. (1998), 'Deliberation as Discussion', in J. Elster (ed.), *Deliberative Democracy*, Cambridge: Cambridge University Press.

Festinger, L. (1957), *A Theory of Cognitive Dissonance*, Stanford, CA: Stanford University Press.

Fishkin, J. (2009), *When the People Speak: Deliberative Democracy and Public Consultation*, Oxford: Oxford University Press.

Frederick, S., Loewenstein, G. and O'Donoghue, T. (2002), 'Time Discounting and Time Preference: A Critical Review', *Journal of Economic Literature*, 40: 351–401.

Freedman, J.L. and Fraser, S.C. (1966), 'Compliance without Pressure: the Foot-in-the-Door Technique', *Journal of Personality and Social Psychology*, 4: 195–202.

Fung, A. (2003a), 'Deliberative Democracy, Chicago Style: Grass-roots Governance in Policing and Public Education', in A. Fung and E. O. Wright (eds), *Deepening Democracy*, London: Verso.

Fung, A. (2003b), 'Survey Article: Recipes for Public Spheres: Eight Institutional Design Choices and their Consequences', *Journal of Political Philosophy*, 11: 338–67.

Fung, A. (2006), *Empowered Participation: Reinventing urban Democracy*, Princeton, NJ: Princeton University Press.

Fung, A. and Wright, E. (2003), *Deepening Democracy: Institutional Innovations in Empowered Participatory Governance*, London: Verso.

Gallup Organization (1993), *The American Public's Attitude toward Organ Donation and Transplantation*, Princeton, NJ: Gallup Organization.

Geller, E.S., Kalsher, M.J., Rudd, J.R. and Lehman, G.R. (1989), 'Promoting Safety Belt Use on a University Campus: an Integration of Commitment and Incentive Strategies', *Journal of Applied Social Psychology*, 19: 3–19.

Gerber, A.S. and Green, D.P. (2000), 'The Effects of Canvassing, Telephone Calls, and Direct Mail on Voter Turnout: a Field Experiment', *American Political Science Review*, 94: 653–63.

Gerber, E.R. and Phillips, J.H. (2002), 'Land Use Policy: Institutional Design and the Responsiveness of Representative Government', Paper presented at the Midwest Political Science Association Annual Meeting, Chicago, April.

Gerber, A.S., Green, D.P. and Shachar, R. (2003), 'Voting May be Habit-forming: Evidence from a Randomised Field Experiment', *American Journal of Political Science*, 47: 540–50.

Gerber, A.S. Green, D.P. and Kaplan, E.H. (2004), 'The Illusion of Learning From Observational Research', in I. Shapiro, R.M. Smith and T. Masoud (eds), *Problems and Methods in the Study of Politics*, Cambridge: Cambridge University Press.

Gerber, A.S., Green, D.P. and Larimer, C.W. (2008), 'Social Pressure and Voter Turnout: Evidence from a Large-scale Field Experiment', *American Political Science Review*, 102: 33–47.

Gerring, J. (2006), *Case Study Research: Principles and Practices*, Cambridge: Cambridge University Press.

Goodin, R. (2004), 'Heuristics of Public Administration', in Mie Auger and James G. March (eds), *Models of a Man. Essays in Memory of Herbert A Simon*, Cambridge: MIT Press

Green, D.P. and Gerber, A.S. (2002), 'Reclaiming the Experimental Tradition in Political Science', in H. Milner and I. Katznelson (eds), *State of the Discipline*, vol. 111, New York, NY: Norton.

Green, D.P. and Gerber, A.S. (2003), 'The Underprovision of Experiments in Political Science', *ANNALS of the American Academy of Political and Social Science*, 589: 94–112.

Green, D.P. and Gerber, A.S. (2008), *Get Out the Vote!: How to Increase Voter Turnout*, 2nd edition, Washington, DC: Brookings Institution Press.

Greenberg, D.H., Linkz, D. and Mandell, M. (2003), *Social Experimentation and Public Policy Making*, Washington, DC: Urban Institute Press.

Greenwald, A., Carnot, C., Beach, R. and Young, B. (1987), 'Increasing Voting Behavior by Asking People if they Expect to Vote', *Journal of Applied Psychology*, 72: 315–18.

Grose, C.R. and Russell, C.A. (2009), 'Avoiding the Vote: A Theory and Field Experiment the Social Costs of Public Participation', Working paper, Nashville, TN: Vanderbilt University.

Gutmann, A. and Thompson, D. (1996), *Democracy and Disagreement*, Cambridge, MA: Belknap Press.

Halpern, D. (2005), *Social Capital*, Cambridge: Polity.

Halpern, D. (2010), *The Hidden Wealth of Nations*, Cambridge: Polity.

Harburgh, W.T. (1998), 'What Do Donations Buy? A Model of Philanthropy Based on Prestige and Warm Glow', *Journal of Public Economics*, 67: 269–84.

Harder, M.K., Woodard, R. and Bench, M.L. (2006), 'Two Measured Parameters Correlated to Participation Rates in Kerbside Recycling Schemes in the UK', *Environmental Management*, 37: 487–95.

Hirst, P. (1993), *Associative Democracy: New Forms of Economic and Social Governance*, Cambridge: Polity.

House, J.S. (1981), *Work, Stress and Social Support*, Reading, MA: Addison-Wesley.

Huck, S. and Rasul, I. (2008), *Comparing Charitable Fundraising Schemes: Evidence From a Natural Field Experiment*, ELSE Working Papers (274), London: ESRC Centre for Economic Learning and Social Evolution.

Improvement and Development Agency (2009), *In Shape for Success? Chief Executives' perspectives on achieving culture change in local government*, London: Improvement and Development Agency.

Janssen, D. and Kies, R. (2005), 'Online Forums and Deliberative Democracy', *Acta Politica*, 40: 317–35.

John, P. (2009), 'Can Citizen Governance Redress the Representative Bias of Political Participation?', *Public Administration Review*, 69: 494–503.

John, P. (2011), *Making Policy Work*, London: Routledge.

John, P. and Brannan, T. (2006), 'How to Mobilise the Electorate: Lessons from the University of Manchester "Get Out the Vote" Experiment', *Representation*, 42: 209–21.

John, P. and Brannan, T. (2008), 'How Different are Telephoning and Canvassing? A Get Out the Vote Field Experiment in the UK 2005 General Election', *British Journal of Political Science*, 38: 565–74.

John. P., Fieldhouse, E. and Liu, H. (2011), 'How Civic is the Civic Culture? Explaining Community Participation Using 2005 English Citizenship Survey', *Political Studies*, 59: 230-252.

Johnson, E.J. and Goldstein, D. (2003), 'Do Defaults Save Lives?', *Science*, 302: 1338–9.

Jones, B. (2001), *Politics and the Architecture of Choice: Bounded Rationality and Governance*, Chicago, IL: University of Chicago Press.

Joss, S. and Durant, J. (eds) (1995), *Public Participation in Science: The Role of Consensus Conferences in Europe*, London: Science Museum.

Jowell, R. (2003), *Trying it Out. The Role of 'Pilots' in Policy-Making*, London: Cabinet Office.

Kahneman, D. and Tversky A. (1979), 'Prospect Theory: An Analysis of Decisions Under Risk', *Econometrica*, 47: 313–27.

Kahneman, D., Knetsch, J.L. and Thaler, R.H. (1990), 'Experimental Tests of the Endowment Effect and the Coase-theorem', *Journal of Political Economy*, 98: 1325–48.

Katzev, R.D. and Pardini, A.U. (1987), 'The Comparative Effectiveness of Reward and Commitment Approaches in Motivating Community Recycling', *Journal of Environmental Systems*, 17: 93–114.

Kendall, J. (2009), *The Value of Volunteering in Europe in the Noughties*, Birmingham: Third Sector Research Centre.

King, G., Keohane, R. and Verba, S. (1994), *Designing Social Inquiry: Scientific Inference in Qualitative Research*, Princeton, NJ: Princeton University Press.

Kingdon, J. (1995), *Agendas, Alternatives and Public Policies*, New York, NY: Harper Collins.

Laibson, D. (1997), 'Golden Eggs and Hyperbolic Discounting', *Quarterly Journal of Economics*, 112: 443–77.

Lijphart, A. (1997), 'Unequal Participation: Democracy's Unresolved Dilemma', *American Political Science Review*, 91: 1–14.

Local Government Association (2008), *The Reputation of Local Government*, London: Local Government Association.

Lowndes, V., Pratchett, L.P. and Stoker, G. (2001), 'Trends in Public Participation: Part 2 – Citizen Perspectives', *Public Administration*, 79: 452–3.

Lowndes, V. Pratchett, L. and Stoker, G. (2006), 'Diagnosing and Remedying the Failings of Official Participation Schemes: the CLEAR Framework', *Social Policy and Society*, 5: 281–91.

Ludwig, T., Buchholz, C. and Clarke, S. (2005), 'Using Social Marketing to Increase the Use of Helmets Among Bicyclists', *Journal of American College Health*, 54: 51–8.

Lunch, C. and Lunch, N. (2006), *Insights into Participatory Video: A Handbook for the Field*, Oxford: InsightShare, http://insightshare.org/resources/pv-handbook [accessed 16 May 2011].

Lupia, A. and Sin, G. (2003), 'Which Public Goods are Endangered? How Evolving Communication Technologies Affect the Logic of Collective Action', *Public Choice*, 117: 315–31.

Luskin, R.C., Fishkin, J.S. and Iyengar, S. (2006), 'Considered Opinions on US Foreign Policy: Face-to-Face versus Online Deliberative Polling', Paper available from the Center for Deliberative Democracy, Stanford, CA: Stanford University, http://cdd.stanford.edu/research/index.html [16 May 2011].

Lyas, J.K., Shaw, P.J. and Van Vugt, M. (2004), 'Provision of Feedback to Promote Householders' Use of a Kerbside Recycling Scheme – A Social Dilemma Perspective', *Journal of Solid Waste Technology*, 30: 7–18.

Macedo, S. (ed.) (1999), *Deliberative Politics: Essays on Democracy and Disagreement*, Oxford: Oxford University Press.

McKenzie-Mohr, D. (2000), 'Promoting Sustainable Behaviour: An Introduction to Community-based Social Marketing', *Journal of Social Issues*, 56: 543–54.

McKenzie-Mohr, D. and Smith, W. (1999), *Fostering Sustainable Behavior: An Introduction to Community-Based Social Marketing*, Gabriola Island, Canada: New Society Publishers.

Mansbridge, J., Hartz-Karp, J., Amengual, M. and Gastil, J. (2006), 'Norms of Deliberation: An Inductive Study', *Journal of Public Deliberation*, 2: Article 7, http://services.bepress.com/jpd/vol2/iss1/art7 [16 May 2011].

March, J. and Olsen, J. (1989), *Rediscovering Institutions*, New York, NY: Free Press.

Micheletti, M. (2010), *Political Virtue and Shopping: Individuals, Consumerism, and Collective Action*, New York, NY: Palgrave Macmillan.

Miller, D. (1992), 'Deliberative Democracy and Social Choice', *Political Studies (Special Issue: Prospects for Democracy)*, 40: 54–67.

Mohan, J. (2011), 'Is there a British "Civic Core"? Evidence from the Citizenship Survey on Patterns of Volunteering, Donations to Charity, and Civic Participation', *Third Sector Research Centre Working Paper*, forthcoming, http:www.tsrc.ac.uk [16 May 2011].

Morales, L. (2009), *Joining Political Organisations: Institutions, Mobilisation and Participation in Western Democracies*, Colchester: ECPR Press.

Neblo, M., Esterling, K., Kennedy, R., Lazer, D. and Sokhey, A. (2010), 'Who Wants to Deliberate – and Why?', *American Political Science Review*, 104: 566–83.

New, W., Solomon, M., Dingwall, R. and McHale, J. (1994), *A Question of Give and Take. Improving the Supply of Donor Organs for Transplantation*, London: King's Fund.

Newton, R., Pierce, A., Richardson, L. and Williams, M. (2010), *Citizens and Local Decision-making: What Drives Feelings of Influence?*, London: Urban Forum.

Nickerson, D. (2006), 'Volunteer Phone Calls Can Increase Turnout: Evidence from Eight Field Experiments', *American Politics Research*, 34: 271–92.

Nomura, H., Cotterill, S. and John, P. (2010), 'The Use of Feedback to Enhance Environmental Outcomes: a Randomised Controlled Trial of a Food Waste Scheme. *Local Environment*, forthcoming.

Norris, P. (2001), *Digital Divide: Civic Engagement, Information Poverty, and the Internet Worldwide*, Cambridge: Cambridge University Press.

O'Donoghue, T. and Rabin, M. (1999), 'Doing It Now or Later', *American Economic Review*, 89: 103–24.

Oliver, P. (1980), 'Rewards and Punishments as Selective Incentives for Collective Action: Theoretical Investigations', *American Journal of Sociology*, 85: 1356–75.

Oostveen, A.-M. and van den Besselaar, P. (2004), 'Security as Belief: User's Perceptions on the Security of Electronic Voting Systems', in A. Prosser and R. Krimmer (eds), *Electronic Voting in Europe: Technology, Law, Politics and Society*, Bonn: Gesellschaft für Informatik.

Oostveen, A.-M. and van den Besselaar, P. (2006), 'Non-Technical Risks of Remote Electronic Voting', in A.-V. Anttiroiko and M. Malkia (eds), *The Encyclopedia of Digital Government*, Hershey, PA: Idea Group Inc.

Osborne, D. and Gaebler, T. (1993), *Reinventing Government: How the Entrepreneurial Spirit is Transforming the Public Sector*, New York, NY: Penguin.

Panagopoulos, C. (2010), 'Affect, Social Pressure and Prosocial Motivation: Field Experimental Evidence of the Mobilizing Effects of Pride, Shame and Publicizing Voting Behavior', *Political Behavior*, 32: 369–86.

Pattie, C. and Seyd, P. (2003), 'Citizenship and Civic Engagement: Attitudes and Behaviour in Britain', *Political Studies*, 51: 443–68.

Pattie, C., Seyd, P. and Whiteley, P. (2005), *Citizenship in Britain: Values, Participation and Democracy*, Cambridge: Cambridge University Press.

Pawson, R. and Tilly, N. (1997), *Realistic Evaluation*, London: Sage.

Peters, B.G. (1998), *Comparative Politics. Theory and Methods*, London: Macmillan.

Petrosino A., Turpin-Petrosino, C. and Buehler J. (2003), 'Scared Straight and Other Juvenile Awareness Programs for Preventing Juvenile Delinquency: A Systematic Review of the Randomised Experimental Evidence', *Annals of the American Academy of Political and Social Science* 589: 41–62.

Phillips, A. (1991), *Engendering Democracy*, Cambridge: Polity.

Phillips, A. (1995), *The Politics of Presence*, Oxford: Oxford University Press.

Prabhakar, R. (2010), 'Nudge, nudge, say no more', *Guardian*, 9 March.

Price, V. (2006), 'Citizens Deliberating Online: Theory and Some Evidence', in T. Davies (ed.), *Online Deliberation: Design, Research, and Practice*, Chicago, IL: University of Chicago Press.

Przeworski, A. and Teune, H. (1970), *The Logic of Comparative Social Inquiry*, New York, NY: Wiley-Interscience.

Putnam, R. (1993), *Making Democracy Work*, Princeton, NJ: Princeton University Press.

Putnam, R. (2000), *Bowling Alone: The Collapse and Revival of American Community*, New York, NY: Simon and Schuster.

Putnam, R. and Pharr, S. (2000), *Disaffected Democracies: What's Troubling the Trilateral Countries?*, Princeton, NJ: Princeton University Press.

Quinn, M.T., Alexander, G.C., Hollingsworth, D., O'Connor, K.G. and Meltzer, D. (2006), 'Design and Evaluation of a Workplace Intervention to Promote Organ Donation', *Progress in Transplantation*, 16: 253–9.

Read, A.D. (1999), 'A Weekly Doorstep Recycling Collection, I Had No Idea We Could! Overcoming the Local Barriers to Participation', *Resources, Conservation and Recycling*, 26: 217–49.

Reams, M.A. and Ray, B. (1993), 'The Effects of Three Prompting Methods on Recycling Participation Rates – A Field-study', *Journal of Environmental Systems*, 22: 371–9.

Reno, R.R., Cialdini, R.B. and Kallgren, C.A. (1993), 'The Transsituational Influence of Social Norms', *Journal of Personality and Social Psychology*, 64: 104–12.

Reubsaet, A., Brug, J., Nijkamp, M.D., Candel, M.J.J.M., Hooff, J.P. van and Borne, H.W. van den (2005), 'The Impact of an Organ Donation Registration

Information Program for High School Students in the Netherlands', *Social Science and Medicine*, 60: 1479–86.

Richardson, L. (2008), *DIY Community Action. Neighbourhood Problems and Community Self-help*, Bristol: Policy Press.

Richardson, L. and John, P. (2011), 'Who Listens to the Grassroots? A Field Experiment on Informational Lobbying in the UK', unpublished paper.

Rithalia, A., McDaid, C., Suekarran, S., Norman, G., Myers, L. and Sowden, A. (2009), 'A Systematic Review of Presumed Consent Systems for Deceased Organ Donation', *Health Technology Assessment*, 13: 26, DOI: 10.3310/hta1326.

Rogers, B. (2004), *Lonely Citizens, Report of the Working Party on Active Citizenship*, London: IPPR.

Roth, A.E. (1995) 'Introduction to Experimental Economics', in J.H. Kagel and A. E. Roth (eds), *The Handbook of Experimental Economics*, Princeton, NJ: Princeton University Press.

Sack, W. (2005), 'Discourse Architecture and Very Large-scale Conversation', in R. Latham and S. Sassen (eds), *Digital Formations: IT and New Architectures in the Global Realm*, Princeton, NJ: Princeton University Press.

Samuelson, W. and Zeckhauser, R. (1988), 'Status Quo Bias in Decision Making', *Journal of Risk and Uncertainty*, 1: 7–59.

Sartori, G. (1987), *The Theory of Democracy Revisited*, Chatham, NJ: Chatham House.

Saward, M. (2001), 'Making Democratic Connections: Political Equality, Deliberation and Direct Democracy', *Acta Politica*, 36: 361–79.

Schwartz, D., Chang. J. and Lee, M. (2005), 'Instrumentation and Innovation in Design Experiments: Taking the Turn towards Efficiency', unpublished paper.

Schultz, P.W. (1998), 'Changing Behaviour with Normative Feedback Interventions: A Field Experiment on Kerbside Recycling', *Basic and Applied Psychology*, 21: 25–36.

Schultz, P.W., Nolan, J.M., Cialdini, R.B., Goldstein, N.J. and Griskevicius, V. (2007), 'The Constructive, Destructive and Reconstructive Power of Social Norms', *Psychological Science*, 18: 429–34.

Setälä, M., Grönlund, K. and Herne, K, (2007), 'Comparing Voting and Common Statement Treatments: A Citizen Deliberation Experiment', paper prepared for the American Political Science Association's Annual Meeting, Chicago.

Shadish, W.R., Cook, T.D. and Campbell, D.T. (2002), *Experimental and Quasi-Experimental Designs for Generalised Causal Inference*, Boston, MA: Houghton Mifflin.

Shapiro, I. (2005), *The Flight from Reality in the Human Sciences*, Princeton, NJ: Princeton University Press.

Shapiro, I.R., Smith, M. and Masoud, T. (eds) (2004), *Problems and Methods in the Study of Politics*, Cambridge: Cambridge University Press.

Shaw, P.J. (2008), 'Nearest Neighbour Effects in Kerbside Household Waste Recycling Resources', *Conservation and Recycling*, 52: 775–84.

Shaw, P.J. and Maynard, S.J. (2008), 'The Potential of Financial Incentives to Enhance Householders' Kerbside Recycling Behaviour', *Waste Management*, 28: 1732–41.

Shaw, P.J., Lyas, J.K., Maynard, S.J. and Van Vugt, M. (2007), 'On the Relationship Between Set-out Rates and Participation Ratios as a Tool for Enhancement of Curbside Household Waste Recycling', *Journal of Environmental Management*, 83: 34–43.

Simon, H. (1945/1997), *Administrative Behavior*, New York, NY: Free Press.

Simon, H. (1996), *The Sciences of the Artificial*, Cambridge, MA: MIT Press.

Sirianni, C. (2009), *Investing in Democracy: Engaging Citizens in Collaborative Governance*, Washington, DC: Brookings.

Smith, G. (2005), *Beyond the Ballot: 57 Democratic Innovations from Around the World*, London: Power Inquiry, http://www.powerinquiry. org/publications/documents/BeyondtheBallot_000.pdf [accessed 16 May 2011].

Smith, G. (2009), *Democratic Innovations: Designing Institutions for Citizen Participation*, Cambridge: Cambridge University Press.

Smith, J., Gerber, A. and Orlich, A. (2003), 'Self-Prophecy Effects and Voter Turnout', *Political Psychology*, 24: 593–604.

Spital, A. (1995), 'Mandated Choice: A Plan to Increase Public Commitment to Organ Donation', *Journal of the American Medical Association*, 273: 504–6.

Spital, A. (1996), 'Mandated Choice for Organ Donation: Time to Give It a Try', *Annals of Internal Medicine*, 125: 66–9.

Standards for England (2009), *Public Perceptions of Ethics*, Manchester: Standards for England.

Stoker, G. (2006), *Why Politics Matters*, Basingstoke: Palgrave Macmillan.

Stoker, G. and Greasley, S. (2008), 'Mayors and Urban Governance: Developing a Facilitative Leadership Style?', *Public Administration Review*, 720–28.

Stoker, G. and John, P. (2009), 'Design Experiments: Engaging Policy Makers in the Search for Evidence About What Works', *Political Studies*, 57: 337–73.

Stutzer, A., Goette, L. and Zehnder, M. (2006), 'Active Decisions and Pro-Social Behaviour: A Field Experiment in Blood Donation', *Working Paper No. 279*, Institute for Empirical Research in Economics, Zurich: University of Zurich.

Sunstein, C.R. (2001), *Republic.com*, Princeton, NJ: Princeton University Press.

Tajfel, H. and Turner, J.C. (1986), 'The Social Identity Theory of Inter-group Behavior', in S. Worchel and L.W. Austin (eds), *Psychology of Intergroup Relations*, Chicago, IL: Nelson-Hall.

Tajfel, H., Billig, M., Bundy, R.P. and Flament, C. (1971), 'Social Categorization and Intergroup Behaviour', *European Journal of Social Psychology*, 1: 149–78.

Thaler, R.H. (1980), 'Toward a Positive Theory of Consumer Choice', *Journal of Economic Behavior and Organization*, 1: 39–60.

Thaler, R.H. and Bernartzi, S. (2004), 'Save More Tomorrow: Using Behavioural Economics to increase Employee Saving, *Journal of Political Economy*, 112: 164–87.

Thaler, R.H. and Sunstein, C.R. (2008), *Nudge: Improving Decisions about Health, Wealth and Happiness*, New Haven, CT, and London: Yale University Press.

Thomas, C. (2006), *Recycle for Hampshire – Campaign Evaluation Report*.

Timlett, R.E. and Williams, I.D. (2008), 'Public Participation and Recycling Performance in England: A Comparison of Tools for Behavior Change, *Resources Conservation and Recycling*, 52: 622–34.

Torgerson, D. and Torgerson, C. (2008), *Designing Randomised Trials*, Basingstoke: Palgrave.

Tucker, P. (1999), 'Normative Influences in Household Waste Recycling', *Journal of Environmental Planning and Management*, 42: 63–82.

UK Transplant (2008), *UK Transplant Activity Report 2007–2008*, London: NHS Blood and Transplant.

Verba, S., Schlozman, K.L. and Brady, H. (1995), *Voice and Equality: Civic Voluntarism in American Politics*, Cambridge, MA: Harvard University Press.

Verba, S., Nie, N. and Kim, J. (1978), *Participation and Political Equality*, Cambridge: Cambridge University Press.

Vinokur, A.D., Merion, R.M., Couper, M.P., Jones, E.G. and Dong, Y. (2006), 'Educational Web-Based Intervention for High School Students to Increase Knowledge and Promote Positive Attitudes Toward Organ Donation', *Health Education Behaviour*, 33: 773.

Warren, M. and Pearse, H. (eds) (2008), *Designing Deliberative Democracy: The British Columbia Citizens' Assembly*, Cambridge: Cambridge University Press.

Waste and Resources Action Programme (2006a), *Step by Step Guide to Door–to-door Canvassing*, http://www.wrap.org.uk [accessed 7 March 2008].

Waste and Resources Action Programme (2006b), *Improving the Performance of Waste Diversion Schemes: A Good Practice Guide to Monitoring and Evaluation*, http://www.wrap.org.uk [accessed 7 March 2008].

Williams, J.W. (2007), 'The Power of Local Political Debates to Influence Prospective Voters: An Experiment at the Congressional Level', American Political Science Association – Panel on Congressional Campaigns and the Media, Chicago, IL.

Wilson, C.D.H. and Williams, I.D. (2007), 'Kerbside Collection: A Case Study From the North-west of England', *Resources Conservation and Recycling*, 52: 381–94.

Woodward, R., Bench, M., Harder, M.K. (2005), 'The Development of a

UK Kerbside Scheme Using Known Practice', *Journal of Environmental Management*, 75: 115–27.

Wright, S. and Street, J. (2007), 'Democracy, Deliberation and Design: the Case of Online Discussion Forums', *New Media and Society*, 9: 849–69.

Xenos, M. and Kyoung, K. (2008), 'Rocking the Vote and More: An Experimental Study of the Impact of Youth Political Portals', *Journal of Information Technology and Politics*, 5: 175–89.

# Index